LEADER OF LEADERS

THE HANDBOOK FOR PRINCIPALS ON THE CULTIVATION, SUPPORT, AND IMPACT OF TEACHER-LEADERS

Hal Portner

William E. Collins

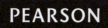

Boston   Columbus   Indianapolis   New York   San Francisco   Upper Saddle River
Amsterdam   Cape Town   Dubai   London   Madrid   Milan   Munich   Paris   Montreal   Toronto
Delhi   Mexico City   Sao Paulo   Sydney   Hong Kong   Seoul   Singapore   Taipei   Tokyo

Vice President and Editorial Director:
Jeffery W. Johnston
Senior Acquisitions Editor: Meredith Fossel
Editorial Assistant: Krista Slavicek
Vice President, Director of Marketing: Margaret Waples
Senior Marketing Manager: Christine Gatchell
Senior Managing Editor: Pamela D. Bennett
Production Project Manager: Carrie Mollette
Senior Art Director: Jayne Conte

Cover Designer: Karen Noferi
Cover Art: Carly Hennigan/Fotolia
Media Project Manager: Noelle Chun
Full-Service Project Management: Peggy Kellar
Composition: Aptara®, Inc.
Printer/Binder: Courier/Westford
Cover Printer: Courier/Westford
Text Font: ITC Garamond Std Light

Credits and acknowledgments for material borrowed from other sources and reproduced, with permission, in this textbook appear on the appropriate page within the text.

Every effort has been made to provide accurate and current Internet information in this book. However, the Internet and information posted on it are constantly changing, so it is inevitable that some of the Internet addresses listed in this textbook will change.

Page iii, Courtesy of William E. Collins

Library of Congress Cataloging-in-Publication Data is available upon request.

10 9 8 7 6 5 4 3 2 1

PEARSON

ISBN 10:   0-13-273641-1
ISBN 13: 978-0-13-273641-1

This book is dedicated to Dale Brubaker, Professor Emeritus,
University of North Carolina, Greensboro,
who passed away June 6, 2013.

Dr. Brubaker's definition of leaders as those who "use [their]
talents to help others identify and use their talents" is the
cornerstone of the authors' concept of Leader of Leaders.

ABOUT THE AUTHORS

Hal Portner is a former public school teacher and administrator. He was also a member of the Connecticut State Department of Education where, among other responsibilities, he served as coordinator of the Connecticut Institute for Teaching and Learning and worked closely with school districts to develop and carry out professional development and teacher evaluation plans and programs. In addition, he served as a professional development consultant for the faculty of Holyoke (MA) Community College and as a master mentoring evaluator for the University of Massachusetts-Dartmouth's Project SUCCESS. Hal develops and facilitates online college courses, develops training materials, trains mentors and

Authors Hal Portner (left) and William "Bill" E. Collins (right)

coaches, facilitates the development of new teacher induction programs, and presents to and consults with school districts and other educational organizations and institutions. He is the author of 10 published books and over 80 articles and is a member of the editorial board of an international peer-review journal. Visit Hal on the web at www.portner.us/.

Bill Collins received his doctorate in educational leadership from Boston College. He serves as the coordinator of the Educational Leadership Program at St. Lawrence University. Bill was a school principal for a decade, most recently at the William E. Norris School located in Southampton, Massachusetts, where teacher-leadership is an integral part of the school's culture. Bill is the founder of the Pioneer Valley Literacy Conference, and he presents on school culture topics including principal evaluation, new teacher induction and mentoring, and teacher-leadership. In the past, Bill has been a middle school guidance counselor, assistant principal, and private school principal. This is his first book. In Bill's spare time, he sails small boats throughout the Northeast. Bill resides in Upstate New York with his wife Diane and their two daughters, Mary Catherine and Julianna.

ACKNOWLEDGMENTS

To our wives, DianeMarie Collins and Mary Portner. Thank you for your unrelenting inspiration, wisdom, support, and sacrifice. It can be truly said that every day, in every way, they prove they are leaders of leaders.

To our children, Mary Catherine and Julianna Collins, Gail Slusarski, Amy Anaya, Cynthia Portner, and Tary Coppola. You make us proud.

To Roland Barth, who in the early 1990s autographed a copy of his book *Improving Schools from Within* for co-author Hal Portner, with the phrase "To a leader of leaders." Roland's writings, coupled with the wording of his autograph, contributed to the inspiration for this book.

To our editors, Stephen Dragin and Meredith Fossel, and their staff at Pearson. Their vision, guidance, and professionalism are embedded in the concept as well as the organization and production of this book.

And last, but certainly not least, to the many dedicated and professional school administrators and teacher-leaders (too many to list here, but you know who you are) with whom we have had the honor and privilege to work and get to know. You are the protagonists of this journey.

The authors also wish to express their appreciation for those individuals who reviewed the manuscript throughout its development: Christopher Amos, University of West Florida; Douglas Clark, Indiana Wesleyan University; Judith Docekal, Loyola University; Sandra C. Harrison, Mosley High School; Scott Roberts, Laredo Independent School District; Mary Joy Rose, Westerville South High School; Jason P. Sherlock, Bayard Rustin High School; and Misti Williams, UNC Greensboro.

BRIEF CONTENTS

Introduction   1

SECTION I   The School Administration   9

Chapter 1   Becoming a More Powerful Leader Through Shared Leadership   10

Chapter 2   A Bountiful Garden   19

Chapter 3   A Leader of Leaders   30

SECTION II   The Teacher as Leader   41

Chapter 4   Who Are Teacher-Leaders?   42

Chapter 5   Where and How Teachers-Leaders Lead   54

Chapter 6   Learning to Lead   68

SECTION III   The Leader of Leader Culture   75

Chapter 7   Shaping School Culture: We Don't Know What We Don't Know   76

Chapter 8   School Climate and Culture   88

Chapter 9   Building Sustainability   99

Conclusion   113

Appendices

Appendix A   Suggested Reading for Those Interested in Additional Study about High-Performance Work Systems   118

Appendix B   Commission on Effective Teachers and Teaching   119

Appendix C   Teacher Leadership Exploratory Consortium   120

Appendix D   Model Standards for Teacher Leadership   122

References   126

Index   138

CONTENTS

INTRODUCTION 1

SECTION I **The School Administration** 9

Chapter 1 **BECOMING A MORE POWERFUL LEADER THROUGH SHARED LEADERSHIP** 10

What We Know Versus What We Do 10

CASE STUDY: Principal Roberta 11

Coping with the Changing Role of the Principal 12

A Change of Perspective Toward Shared Leadership 12

CASE STUDY: Laurie H. 14

In Summary 18

Chapter Discussion Questions 18

Chapter 2 **A BOUNTIFUL GARDEN** 19

CASE STUDY: Principal Roberta's Story—Continued 19

Finding Common Ground 21

Celebrating Wins 22

Principal Paradigm Shifting 22

The Silent Conductor 23

Vantage Point and Perspective 24

Building Collective Efficacy 25

Not Sowing More Than You Can Reap 25

Building Capacity 25

Common Findings Emerge from Teacher-Leader Research 26

In Summary 29

Chapter Discussion Questions 29

Chapter 3 **A LEADER OF LEADERS** 30

Shifting the Principal's Role from "Leader" to "Leader of Leaders" 30

Paradigm Shifting 31

The Journey 32

Principal Roberta's Journey to Leadership 32

The Leader's Role in Building a Team 33

Leaders Create Operating Cultures That Encourage a Sense of Trust 35

Capacity Building Through Teacher Leadership 36

Roberta Empowers the Faculty   37
    CASE STUDY: Kate—The Reading Teacher   38
    CASE STUDY: Morgan—The First Grade Teacher   38
    CASE STUDY: George—The Paraprofessional   38
      In Summary   39
      Chapter Discussion Questions   39

SECTION II The Teacher as Leader   41

Chapter 4 WHO ARE TEACHER-LEADERS?   42
Teachers as Leaders in Their Own Classrooms   44
Teachers as Leaders Beyond the Classroom   46
What Motivates a Teacher-Leader?   47
Barriers to Teacher Leadership   47
Do Unions Present a Barrier to Teacher Leadership?   50
Overcoming Barriers   50
Teacher-Leadership Behaviors   51
    In Summary   52
    Chapter Discussion Questions   53

Chapter 5 WHERE AND HOW TEACHER-LEADERS LEAD   54
Teachers Exercise Leadership Around Issues of School Practices and Policies   55
Teacher-Leaders Work with Individual Colleagues   56
  A Sequenced Program of Classroom Support   57
Teacher-Leaders Work with School-Based Groups   58
  Professional Learning Communities   59
The Principal's Role in School Teams   61
Teachers Lead in Areas of District or Community Issues and Concerns   63
Teachers Lead Beyond Their School, District, and Community   63
Teacher-Leader Networks   64
    In Summary   66
    Chapter Discussion Questions   67

Chapter 6 LEARNING TO LEAD   68
Teacher-Leader Standards   69
Leadership Development Programs   70
State License Endorsements Recognize Teacher Leadership   72
Mentoring Future Teacher-Leaders   73
    In Summary   73
    Chapter Discussion Questions   74

SECTION III The Leader of Leader Culture   75

Chapter 7   SHAPING SCHOOL CULTURE: WE DON'T KNOW WHAT WE DON'T KNOW   76

"Us" and "Them" Mentality   77

Heroes Need Not Apply   78

Transformational Versus Transactional Leadership   79

Teacher-Leader Lite   80

Principal Roberta Lays the Foundation for a School Culture   81

Demanding Failure   81

Principal Roberta Shares Her Hare-Brained Theory   82

Small Wins   83

Trust Building   84

Situational Awareness   84

One Degree Makes All the Difference   85

In Summary   87

Chapter Discussion Questions   87

Chapter 8   SCHOOL CLIMATE AND CULTURE   88

Defining School Climate and Culture   88

School Climate   89

School Culture   89

The Role of the Principal in Changing School Culture   90

How Principals Influence Climate and Culture   91

Building Unity   92

A Culture of Distributive Leadership   93

A Culture of Trust   93

A Culture of Collective Mindfulness   94

Helping the Teacher-Leaders to Help Themselves   95

Reframing the Perceptions of Leadership   95

Separating the Practice from the Practitioner   96

In Summary   97

Chapter Discussion Questions   98

Chapter 9   BUILDING SUSTAINABILITY   99

Ethical Leadership for the Common Good   100

Systemic Approach   101

Self-Renewal   102

Servant Leadership   104

Sustainability   105

Differing Perspectives Make for a Stronger Shared Vision 108
Succession Planning 108
The Fruits of Principal Roberta's Sustainability Planning 109
    In Summary 110
    Chapter Discussion Questions 111

Conclusion 113

Appendices

Appendix A   Suggested Reading for Those Interested in Additional Study about
                High-Performance Work Systems 118
Appendix B   Commission on Effective Teachers and Teaching 119
Appendix C   Teacher Leadership Exploratory Consortium 120
Appendix D   Model Standards for Teacher Leadership 122

References 126

Index 138

Introduction

The word "principal" is derived from the Latin word *principalis*, meaning first or highest in rank. Also from the Latin, the word *educare*, the source of "educator," means to lead out of. By definition, then, educators lead and principals are leaders of leaders. This book is about the principal as the leader of leaders, the teacher-leaders they lead, and the culture that encourages and supports the emergence and development of teacher-leaders. It is our experience as well as our belief that if you don't create a culture, you're going to get one anyway. Therefore, this book is also about the function of the building principal as the catalyst for and champion of the kind of culture that encourages and supports the emergence and development of teacher-leaders. We also examine the characteristics, roles, effectiveness, and professional development of teacher-leaders; the barriers and driving forces that impact their effectiveness; and the differences and similarities between formal and informal teacher-leaders.

SOME BACKGROUND

The first public education system documented in the United States was in Massachusetts, where every town in the state was required to provide schools with certified teachers (Weiss, 1992). Along with the increased number of schools came the need for more certified teachers to staff them. As student populations increased, schools became multigraded, requiring onsite supervision. A head or principal teacher was appointed and received additional compensation to manage the school in addition to teaching students. The additional responsibility included such duties as keeping attendance records, distributing school supplies, maintaining the school building, and, in some instances, making fires during the cold season of the year (Campbell, Fleming, Newell, & Bennion, 1987).

By the 1960s, the title "principal teacher" had become simply "principal," and the role had evolved to the point where the principal was considered a "bureaucratic executive who held power in the school" (Shen, 2005, p. 4). Principals approached their responsibilities from a technical point of view, using scientific strategies to achieve measurable outcomes (Beck & Murphy, 1993).

In the archetypical school today, there is still only one leader: the principal. The principal is the individual who directs curriculum and instruction from the top layer of a hierarchy. In such a scenario, the role of the educator (a.k.a. the teacher) is to be led—to accept the need for change, learn new procedures, and follow the principal's directions to carry out those changes. In practice, however, this chain-of-command model rarely happens because "schools, like most organizations, operate as informal networks rather than hierarchies, with most organizational members feeling more connected to a few . . . colleagues than to nominal leaders" (Reeves, 2006). In "Are We Preparing Students for the 21st Century?," the *Metropolitan Life Survey of the American Teacher* (2000) found that many secondary school faculty members felt alienated and that substantial numbers felt "left out of things going on around them at their school" or that "what they think, doesn't count very much at their school" (p. 10). It was apparent, except in unusual cases, that the basic decisions that affect the work lives of teachers and the performance of their students came from on high—from top-down leadership.

Leana (2011) conducted a series of surveys between 2005 and 2007 in elementary schools across New York City. A representative sample of more than 1,000 fourth- and fifth-grade teachers was asked whom they talked to when they had questions or needed advice. Did they go to other teachers, to the school principal, or to the coaches hired by the district specifically to help them to be better math teachers? How much did they trust the source of the advice they received? It was found that in most instances teachers were almost twice as likely to turn to their peers as to the experts designated by the school district and four times more likely to seek advice from one another than from the building principal.

As schools and schooling have become more complex and the expectations of schools have become more demanding, many administrators have come to realize teachers, not principals, are the educators who have daily contact with learners. They understand that teachers are in the best position to make critical real-time and focused decisions about implementing curriculum and providing instruction (Howey, 1988; Livingston, 1992). Because they also recognize the reality of collegial networks and the advantages of collaborative leadership, these principals assign teachers to leadership roles. They also understand that by doing so they retain highly qualified teachers and keep those teachers involved and growing (Dimock & McGree, 1995). It is likely that, in some instances, the motivation for developing teacher-leaders may be more pragmatic than idealistic. Many schools have been impacted by funding issues resulting in cuts in teaching, administrative, and support staff. Schools still are faced with improving test scores, graduation and attendance rates. Some principals realize that they can rely on teacher-leaders to help them achieve these goals.

Encouraging teachers to take on leadership roles even beyond school and district borders is becoming a goal of policy makers. In Iowa, for example, a new teacher compensation system was a key component of former Iowa governor Terry Branstad's education blueprint (2011). It called for replacing the then current system in which compensation is based on how long a teacher has been in the profession and what degrees he or she has obtained with a system of apprentice, career, mentor, and master teachers. It also called for teachers at the master levels to serve as teacher-leaders and devote part of their time as mentors.

Locally, teachers are often invited to apply for nonadministrative leadership positions and are chosen through a selection process. Ideally, they receive training for their new responsibilities through local, regional, or professional association-sponsored professional development opportunities, or via enrollment in college or university graduate education courses.

Teacher-leaders play vital roles in most schools. In many cases, they manage curriculum projects, facilitate teacher study groups, mentor new teachers, provide workshops, and evaluate materials. Shared Leadership is the term used for another expression of teacher involvement in leadership. Shared leadership means that the principal and a group of teachers form a team to build collective responsibility school-wide for students' character development and achievement. Clemson-Ingram and Fessler (1997) anticipated these and other concepts of the teacher-leader when they defined shared leadership as "a variety of roles for classroom teachers in staff development, management, and school improvement."

As a cautionary note, Danielson (2007) points out that when teachers are selected to evaluate other teachers, their colleagues are likely to regard them as "pseudoadministrators." Under a hierarchal structure, assigned teachers may consider themselves to be teacher-representatives as much as teacher-leaders. For example, some teachers may consider committee work or becoming a department chair at their school not as teacher leadership, but as it "being someone's turn" or getting "stuck" with an extra duty for that year.

INFORMAL TEACHER-LEADERS

A newer, more expansive understanding of the role has begun to emerge that mitigates the perception of teacher leading equating with extra duty. Teachers can also lead *informally*. Rather than being assigned or recruited by administrators, informal teacher-leaders take the initiative to lead. They have no positional authority; they emerge spontaneously and organically from the teacher ranks. They do so in ways that result in their being recognized by their colleagues as leaders because of their credibility, expertise, or relationship-building skills. Like assigned or volunteer teacher-leaders, these teachers may offer support to beginning teachers, design and implement staff development activities, write grants to gain needed resources, or act as technology experts within the school—but they do so out of their own motivation and interest.

Many informal teacher-leaders extend their leadership beyond school walls into the community. Teacher-leaders contribute beyond their own school when they make a presentation at a state or national conference, serve on a state standards board, or speak at a local service club as the voice of teachers in the community.

Some teachers even extend their informal leadership beyond their community. For example, Anthony Cody, a science teacher in inner city Oakland, California, not only works with a team of experienced science teacher-coaches who support the many novice teachers in his school district, he also is an active member of the national Teacher-Leaders Network (TLN). On November 2, 2009, on behalf of the TLN, he wrote an *Open Letter to President Obama* (Cody, 2009) in which he questioned some of Secretary of Education Duncan's decisions and urged that the President "hold your Secretary of Education accountable for enacting the vision that you campaigned on." Other teachers followed Cody's lead, and over 100 additional letters were sent to Obama and Duncan. As a result, Cody and 11 other teachers were invited to speak with Secretary Duncan. The conversation took place on May 24, 2010.

Some administrators may possibly feel threatened when teachers emerge as leaders. They may fear that ambitious teacher-leaders will somehow undermine their own authority. Yet, there is nothing in the concept of teacher-leadership that conflicts with the essential role of administrative-leadership. Principals are still responsible for seeing to it that operations run smoothly. They maintain focus on student learning. They are, along with being managers of the building's operations, the instructional leaders of their schools, and they are the voice of the school to the parents and the wider community. Teacher leadership is more about empowering teachers by increasing their access to resources, information, and expertise in order to positively affect school change (Hallinger & Richardson, 1988).

SCHOOL CULTURE

Danielson (2007) points out that even when a principal effectively carries out these responsibilities, "[n]ot every school is hospitable to the emergence of teacher leaders, particularly informal teacher leaders." An emergent teacher-leader may have a creative approach to solving a difficult issue in her school—an approach that requires change. Creative thinking and change imply risk, and risk-taking requires an environment where teachers feel safe and are confident that administrators and other teachers will not criticize them for expressing ideas.

Morgan (1986) reminds us that culture is not imposed on a school. It develops through the course of social interactions. Although informal leaders, by the nature of their passion and actions, have the potential to affect the culture of the school, ultimately, it is the principal who most influences the development of a professional culture that fosters teacher leadership. If teachers look forward to being involved in the ongoing improvement of the school, seek positive engagement with the community, and proactively contribute to the profession, look to the principal as the catalyst.

Bonnie Wilson exemplifies such a principal. Wilson, principal of Baldwin Academy, a K–5 elementary school in La Puente, California, has developed a school culture that supports a vision of high expectations, hope, and success. She creates leaders out of the majority of her staff by seeking out each staff member's strengths and providing them with leadership opportunities in those particular areas. Her leadership fosters a sense of ownership and pride by teachers, and an understanding that all teachers in her school are leaders.

What does a culture like the one in Baldwin Academy look like and how does a principal bring it about? A study of high leadership capacity schools (Lambert, 2005) identified six factors critical to sustained improvement. These factors not only contribute to successes in teaching and learning, they also describe conditions conducive to teacher leadership development and support.

LAMBERT'S CRITICAL FACTORS INDICATIVE OF HIGH LEADERSHIP CAPACITY SCHOOLS

In a study of continuously high performing schools, Lambert (2005) found that as teachers begin to initiate action, take more responsibility for school effectiveness, frame problems, and seek solutions, principals and teacher-leaders become more alike than different. Lambert identified six factors indicative of high leadership capacity schools.

1. The school community's core values must focus its priorities. Democratization and equity must be foremost among these values and are interdependent. Democratization is the means through which staff experience and honor equity. Members of high leadership capacity schools accept responsibility for all students' learning and include all voices.

2. As teacher-leadership grows, principals must let go of some authority and responsibility. When principals lead for sustainability, teachers and principals become more alike than different. They share similar concerns, blend roles, and ask tough questions. They find leadership and credibility within each other through frequent conversations, shared goals, and, ultimately, collective responsibility.

3. Educators must define themselves as learners, teachers, and leaders. How we define leadership determines who will participate. This broad perspective encompasses sharing and distributing leadership. Leadership becomes a form of learning— reciprocal, purposeful learning in community. To learn is to be able to lead. Like children, all adults can learn, all adults can lead.

4. We must invest in each other's learning to create reciprocity. When principals engage teachers in problem solving rather than render them helpless through directives and granting or withholding permission, natural capacities for reciprocity come to life. Dependencies cause us to ask permission, to abdicate responsibilities, and to blame. Learning communities require reciprocity.

5. The first tenet of leadership capacity is "broad-based participation." Schools must create the structures through which participation occurs. Structures for broad-based participation include teams, study groups, vertical communities, and action research teams. These are the settings in which people deepen relationships, alter their beliefs, and become more skillful in the work of leadership. Without these structures, reculturing is unlikely.

6. Districts must negotiate the political landscape to provide professional time and development, a conceptual framework for improvement, and tailored succession practices (fitting the principal to the school). This work requires engaging the board and the community in conversations that build an understanding of lasting school improvement. Without this groundwork, schools continually fight the same battles for time, for professional development, and for selecting principals who can take a school from where it is to where it ought to be without losing momentum or denying the worthy experiences of teacher-leaders. These factors are particularly challenging because they challenge our beliefs and traditional conceptions of leadership, how we relate to each other and ourselves, and how we distribute power and authority. We consistently have called on ordinary people to do extraordinary work, and many times we succeed. We can succeed more often if we understand and implement the tenets of leadership capacity for lasting school improvement. The notion of "lasting" or sustainable improvement may well represent today's major learning edge.

Lambert's findings are consistent with Sergiovanni's notion of leadership density. Sergiovanni (2001) argues that high leadership density means that many people work collaboratively, are trusted with information, participate in decision-making, and contribute to the creation and transfer of knowledge.

Roby (2011, p. 789) notes that when conditions change to enhance school cultures, they move from:

- Total self-interest to sincere interest in helping coworkers
- Just congeniality to collegiality
- Blaming and complaining to accepting and solving
- Just extrinsic and intrinsic motivators to moral motivators
- Primarily contractual relationships to covenantal relationships
- A school of coworkers to a community of learners
- One-way mentorship to two-way mentorship
- Being reactive to becoming proactive
- Little or no involvement in important decision-making to high involvement
- An operational focus to a professional focus

A good leader inspires people to have confidence in the leader. A great leader inspires people to have confidence in themselves.

—ANON.

LEADERSHIP TRAINING

Traditional educational leadership programs in colleges and universities are designed to prepare credentialed school administrators. Guided by recent calls for reform, however, these educational leadership programs are focusing more and more on team building, goal setting, collaborative decision-making, and conflict resolution (Crews & Weakley, 1995), in addition to an increased emphasis on improving student performance. Many programs require students to go through the preparation experience in cohorts, enhancing meaningful and relevant learning as well as fostering a sense of community (Barnett, Basom, Yerkes, & Norris, 2000; Hill, 1995; Kraus & Cordeiro, 1995; Norris & Barnett, 1994). Significant internship experiences, where students integrate practice with new knowledge and receive mentoring from practicing administrators, are among the most highly valued program experiences (Krueger & Milstein, 1995). The national call for accountability of educational institutions has resulted in standards-based reform efforts of educational leadership preparation programs. The initiatives of the Interstate School Leaders Licensure Consortium (ISLLC) and the Educational Leadership Constituent Council (ELCC) are articulated in the Journal of Research for Educational Leaders (Greenlee, 2007) as professional standards for administrator preparation programs. These standards call for preparation of school leaders who have the knowledge and ability to:

- Facilitate the development, articulation, implementation, and stewardship of a school or district vision of learning supported by the school community
- Promote a positive school culture, provide an effective instructional program, apply best practice to student learning, and design comprehensive professional growth plans for staff
- Manage the organization, operations, and resources in a way that promotes a safe, efficient, and effective learning environment
- Collaborate with families and other community members, respond to diverse community interests and needs, and mobilize community resources
- Act with integrity, fairly, and in an ethical manner
- Understand, respond to, and influence the larger political, social, economic, legal, and cultural context
- Participate in an extensive internship

Teachers who want to be school principals enroll in educational leadership programs. Those teachers who want to pursue graduate degrees and remain in the classroom usually enroll in curriculum and instruction programs. Hackney and Henderson (1999), advocating for truly democratic leadership structures, proposed discontinuing the separate graduate education of future administrators and teachers, asserting that if "democratic school leadership is to be made operational in the schools, both teachers and administrators must understand theoretically and practically what that will mean" (p. 72). Based on this and other studies (e.g., McCay, Flora, Hamilton, & Riley, 2001), aspiring administrators and teacher-leaders may require very similar practical and theoretical knowledge bases.

In keeping with this notion, more and more of the participants in educational leadership programs have been those who wish to assume more active roles in education reform and school renewal as teacher-leaders without moving to administration (Greenlee, 2007). Some institutions—Penn State, for example—offer an MEd in Educational Leadership with an option in teacher leadership.

Other colleges and universities, recognizing the expanding number of teacher-leaders who want to remain in the classroom, have instituted separate teacher leadership MEd-granting programs. One example, the University of Central Florida, offers an MEd program in Teacher Leadership that specifically does not prepare students for initial administrative or supervisory certification. The program, as described in the university's 2011–2012 Graduate Catalog, "is designed for certified and experienced educators who want to extend their influence beyond the walls of the classroom, to improve their knowledge and skills in the area of leadership, and who want to develop expertise in leading other educators in curriculum and instructional improvement across subject areas and grade levels."

Another institution, the University of Cincinnati, offers the Master of Education Curriculum & Instruction Teacher Leader program "designed for those active classroom teachers who are interested in assuming a leadership role and added responsibility within their school (or building) but are not interested in becoming a principal."

The Teacher Leadership for Urban Schools is funded by the Ford Foundation and coordinated by The Consortium for Excellence in Teacher Education. The program provides teachers in their 3rd to 11th years of teaching with an opportunity to explore the next stage of their career path, experiment with various forms of educational leadership, and learn effective teacher-leader skills.

State Departments of Education, too, are recognizing the emergence of trained teacher-leaders. The Ohio Department of Education, for example, has established criteria in its 2009 Program Standards, Grades P–12, for a teacher-leader endorsement to its professional teacher license. The endorsement may be issued to an individual who has successfully completed four years of teaching experience, holds a master's degree, has met the program standards, is deemed to be of good moral character, and who has been recommended by the dean or head of teacher education at an institution approved to prepare teachers in Ohio. Some university teacher-leader programs such as the one at Samford University (Birmingham, Alabama) facilitate their state's certification application paperwork for its students.

Especially noteworthy because they emphasize the emergence of grassroots interest in developing both teacher and administrative leadership is the implementation of training and support by local school districts and regional educational collaboratives. Notable examples include:

- The Office of Educator Quality Teacher Leadership Development Program at the Austin Texas Independent School District is designed for teachers who wish to become more informed and effective in roles such as master teacher, instructional team leader, curriculum planner, teacher specialist, or department chair.
- The Montgomery County (Maryland) Public Schools (MCPS) Leadership Development Program (LDP) recruits at the teacher level and prepares aspiring principals via a series of Future Administrators Workshops.

A teacher-leader component designed exclusively for the Knowledge Is Power Program (KIPP) provides training opportunities for teachers to hone their instructional skills while maximizing their leadership potential. KIPP is a network of free, open-enrollment, college-preparatory public schools with teachers in roles such as grade-level chair, department/content chair, Saturday school coordinator, or field lesson coordinator. Each participant in the program, in collaboration with their school leader, picks one of two strands: either research (i.e., skillful teaching), or team leadership and management.

Timpe (2008, July) adds another dimension to leadership when he considers it to be about mission, vision, and values as well as structure, process, and culture. As he puts it, "the mission and, yes, improvement in teacher effectiveness via effective professional development leads to the bottom line of evaluation: the extent it affects student achievement."

Finally, because you are reading this book, we assume that you are someone who is a leader, someone who is going to become a leader, someone who hasn't yet decided whether you want to be a leader, someone who trains and/or otherwise supports leaders, or someone who is just plain curious about teacher-leaders, principals as leaders of leaders, and/or the culture of collaborative leadership in education. If you fit one or more of these demographics, we have written this book for you.

SECTION I

The School Administration

Chapter 1 Becoming a More Powerful Leader Through Shared Leadership
Chapter 2 A Bountiful Garden
Chapter 3 A Leader of Leaders

1 Becoming a More Powerful Leader Through Shared Leadership

If you don't know where you are going, any road will get you there.

—LEWIS CARROLL

First published in 1989, the book *The Seven Habits of Highly Effective People* (Covey, 1989) became an international sensation, ultimately selling more than 25 million copies printed in over 35 languages. Covey's work struck a chord with an audience eager to lead more effective lives. The second of the seven habits is to begin with the end in mind. Likewise, Tighe and Wiggins (2005) list *start with the end in mind* as one of the tenets to follow for educators using their *Understanding by Design* to plan lessons and curriculum. This theme can be found reoccurring throughout literature. There appears to be a universal truth that resonates with those searching to improve personal and professional effectiveness: possessing a clear under-standing of where one wants to end up before beginning is critical to success. There are those who have serendipitously stumbled into success, but perhaps Louis Pasteur put it best: "Chance favors the prepared mind." This advice may seem simple, but why then is it that the ability to stick to our goals can elude so many of us?

WHAT WE KNOW VERSUS WHAT WE DO

The first question for school leaders is "who makes the biggest difference in the school?" Some school administrators fail to see that teachers, not administrators, have the greatest impact on children. While most administrators do realize this, significantly fewer administrators actually put this knowledge into action in a way that exemplifies the understanding that teachers are in the best position to make critical real-time and focused decisions about implementing curriculum and providing instruction.

This is not an unusual school phenomenon. The gap is wide between what is known to work in schools and what is actually practiced in most schools. Schmoker (2006a) points to the gap between established essential practices and the reality existing in schools. Schmoker believes that even teachers and administrators who are aware of best practices do not consistently use or reinforce them.

CASE STUDY

Principal Roberta

Meet an elementary school principal named Roberta. Roberta is a real person; only her name has been changed to preserve her anonymity. We will use Roberta to provide real life examples throughout the text and to illustrate important points.

Roberta began her career in education as a middle school guidance counselor before becoming an administrator. Her first administrative role was as a middle school assistant principal; then she worked as the principal in a 150-pupil kindergarten to Grade 8 (K–8) school; and finally she was the principal of a 550-pupil preK–6 school.

When Roberta was a counselor, she used an allegory about a snake as a means of driving home the importance of keeping one's destination in mind. She found that too many of her adolescent students easily lost sight of their goals. The students not only made choices that did not bring them closer to their goals, but made choices that were downright counterproductive and actually undermined their goals.

Roberta had the students imagine that they were on a lovely hike heading out of town. After about 20 minutes of a slow and steady climb, the town would become visible below, offering a new vantage point. The sun would shine down from the cloudless sky and the students could see all the recognizable landmarks clearly: the school, the movie theater, the fire station, and the hospital. Suddenly, a searing pain just above the ankle would cause the student to look down. Unbelievably, a snake would be slithering away under some rocks; it was evident that the student had just been bitten by a poisonous snake and would need to make some important decisions quickly.

Roberta guided her students ultimately to understand that their first impulse—to take revenge on the snake—would be a waste of valuable time and energy, if their goal was survival. This allegory would then lead her students to see how they were actually choosing the equivalent of chasing the snake in their current situation. Like Roberta's students, no matter how unfair it was to be bitten by the snake, whatever our snake may represent, the time we spend feeling sorry for ourselves, hatching plots of revenge, or otherwise turning our sights away from our ultimate goal only serves to harm us. In order not to be snake chasers, we need to articulate what is important in our personal and professional lives, determine where we are going, and make plans for how to get there.

COPING WITH THE CHANGING ROLE OF THE PRINCIPAL

The fact that student achievement is most impacted by teachers does not make school administrators, such as principals, irrelevant or less important; if anything, it makes them critical to the support of the teacher–student relationship. Effective principals clearly understand and define their role in order to achieve effectiveness. Duignan (2009) supports this notion by maintaining that "school leadership is second only to teaching in influencing what students learn at school" (p. 3). It can be inferred from the work of Goldring et al. (2009) that the principalship and principal leadership matter to the success and/or failure of public school children. The principalship is where the locus of control resides in school systems, and it allows for a common or shared vision; otherwise, teacher-leaders in the school would be leading in their own unique directions.

The principalship has undergone changes over the last 50 years that add many levels of complexity to the role, making it increasingly difficult for any one person to effectively carry out all of the responsibilities. What is the modern principal to do? Kempher and Cooper (2002) describe the modern principal as having to be "all things to all people" and the principal's role as becoming so much more complex in recent years as to demand "a professional, well-educated 'manager.' Because principals work with everyone from the students to the school board president . . ." (p. 33).

In exploration of the evolution of the principal's role from manager to instructional leader and the increased responsibilities and duties that accompany the new demands upon principals, Stronge and Leeper (2012) found that "paradoxically, when principals give power away they oftentimes become more powerful. This enables them to narrow their focus and concentration to factors that contribute directly to school effectiveness" (p. 8). Casavant, Collins, Faginski, McCandless, and Tencza (2012) postulated that trust and distributive leadership were a way for principals to make sense out of the complexity surrounding the role of the modern principalship.

A CHANGE OF PERSPECTIVE TOWARD SHARED LEADERSHIP

If the principalship has become too complex to effectively carry out all its duties, and teachers are positioned to have the most impact on students, then it stands to reason that enlisting the help of teachers to achieve school goals is a logical next step. It can be a difficult step for some principals who have been trained to never admit that they need help or to let others know that they do not possess all of the answers. Wiseman (2010) identifies two styles of leaders. The first is the ineffective leader who always needs to be the smartest person in the room and as such depletes the capability, energy, and intelligence from everyone else. This leader creates a reverse synergy in the organization. The second is the more effective leader who magnifies the capabilities, energies, and intelligence of others, thus creating a synergic win-win organization.

Heifetz (1994) refers to a change in leadership perspective as "getting on the balcony." Leaders need to change their vantage point, and by getting above the fray they gain a perspective that being in the thick of it does not allow. Senge (1990) calls this change in perspective "systems thinking" and an essential component to creating "learning organizations." Senge's second of his five disciplines states that the harder you push, the harder the system pushes back. Simmons (2010) suggests that the solution to the push-back problem "lies in creating new systems to generate new results, not in expecting broken systems to produce the same or better results." Simmons warns leaders, "Push your system and the people in it as hard as you want and you might get short term results, but you will inevitably create new problems and probably never see how your heroic efforts contributed to the mounting malaise."

Stronge and Leeper (2012) found shared leadership was "made coherent through a common culture" and "results in the creation of multiple leaders within a school" (p. 8). The authors saw shared leadership impacting principals and stakeholders in different ways: "[F]or the principal, it lightens the load and provides support" (p. 8), while for the stakeholder, "it highlights the important role that everyone has in guiding and directing the school community toward the vision and goals" (p. 8), viewing decision making as a team effort that, once implemented, more fully allows the principal to act as diagnostician and facilitator.

In the role of diagnostician and facilitator, the principal is better situated to identify and address issues and find solutions. Stronge and Leeper (2012) are quick to point out that the "principal does not relinquish responsibility, rather he/she promotes others, encourages shared decision making, and builds relationships. All of this contributes to a positive school climate" (p. 8). Building relationships takes time, but doing so it lays the groundwork for being able to more productively move the organization in the right direction.

Hattie (2009) identified two types of leadership in which principals engage: *instructional leadership* and *transformational leadership*. Hattie defined instructional leadership as those activities that were more managerial in nature, such as keeping the school free from distraction, creating and publicizing clear learning objectives, and setting clear and high expectations for both teachers and students. Conversely, he defined transformational leadership as the activities in which the principal worked to "engage with their teaching staff in ways that inspire them to new levels of energy, commitment, and moral purpose such that they work collaboratively to overcome challenges and reach ambitious goals" (p. 83).

A Wallace Foundation study (2011) identified five key responsibilities for school principals:

- Shaping a vision of academic success for all students, one based on high standards
- Creating a climate hospitable to education in order that safety, a cooperative spirit, and other foundations of fruitful interaction prevail
- Cultivating leadership in others so that teachers and other adults assume their part in realizing the school vision
- Improving instruction to enable teachers to teach at their best and students to learn at their utmost
- Managing people, data, and processes to foster school improvement

The Wallace study found that the third key responsibility, cultivating leadership in others, was "a central part of being a great leader" (p. 11). This study noted that the principal's "authority does not wane as other's waxes" (p. 7). It also found that "a broad and longstanding consensus in leadership theory holds that leaders in all walks of life and all kinds of organizations, public and private, need to depend on others to accomplish the group's purpose" (pp. 6–7). The Wallace study went on to state that principals and schools are no different from other organizations and their leaders when it comes to cultivating leadership in others. "[The principal] has and need[s] to encourage the development of leadership across the organization . . . Principals who get high marks from teachers for creating a strong climate for instruction in their schools also receive higher marks than other principals for spurring leadership in the faculty" (pp. 6–7).

Sergiovanni (2001) explained that "the principal who insists on being a strong instructional leader, even though teachers are perfectly capable of providing all the necessary leadership, forces teachers into dependent roles and removes opportunities and incentives for them to be self-managers" (p. 67). Marzano, Waters, and McNulty (2005) published a meta-analysis on the relationship between principals' responsibilities and student achievement. They scoured the educational studies conducted from 1978 until 2001 on kindergarten through Grade 12, which included an approximate combined total of 14,000 teachers and 1.4 million students. Their meta-analysis suggested several strong relationships between student achievement and principal responsibility, but the strongest was a principal's situational awareness. Situational awareness was defined as "the extent to which the principal is aware of the details and undercurrents in the running of the school and uses this information to address current and potential problems" (p. 43).

It stands to reason that principals who are situationally aware find themselves better situated to respond and lead than those who do not possess the same level of awareness. If the number one principal activity to influence student achievement is situational awareness, then the next question is "how do principals build situational awareness?" The most situationally aware principals are out of their offices and in the school; they have to be in classrooms and have frequent professional conversations with teachers. As soon as the principal steps out across the threshold of his or her office door, he or she increases effectiveness. The most important action is happening in the classrooms; the further and longer the principal removes himself or herself from that action, the less effective and situationally aware the principal becomes.

The principal, much like an athletic coach or an orchestra conductor, has the advantage of perspective, a piece that teachers often lack. Teachers, in turn, tend to have a better microview that principals can often lack. The trick is to improve everybody's situational awareness by improving the principal's microview and the teachers' macroview. If the teacher knew that the school's copier budget was cut by 12%, then maybe he would make different copying choices and select black and white copies instead of color. This knowledge might prevent him from feeling the principal was being unreasonable by tracking how many color copies each teacher made. If the principal knew that it was essential for a particular lesson to be color-coded and that the teacher was aware of the budget cut, she may be able to turn her attention to matters of greater impact to students.

CASE STUDY

Laurie H.

As the child of two longtime public educators, becoming an educator herself was in Laurie's genes. When Laurie took on her first principalship at a high school, she knew exactly the kind of culture she didn't want to create.

Like most school principals, Laurie began her career as a teacher. In her first teaching position as the newest and youngest member of the faculty at a large urban high school, Laurie was incredulous that no one in the English department mentored her, collaborated with her, or even showed the slightest interest in her instruction; she was left alone to sink or swim on her own. In contrast to her colleagues, Laurie taught with her door wide open, and student work was prominently displayed around the classroom and hung from the ceilings. Fresh from a master's degree program, Laurie was ready and eager in her mid-twenties to connect with students and perfect a teaching style that would engage students in their own learning, yet her principal never observed her—not once! The principal had little idea of what was occurring in Laurie's classroom and the successes that her students were finding. Laurie had to find her own mentors and naturally turned to her veteran educator parents for guidance. Laurie's mother and father fostered her professional development and growth as a new teacher.

Laurie moved on after 3 years in search of a school climate that would meet her needs. She landed a department head job in an affluent suburban school and coached field hockey after school. Laurie soon discovered that while her new principal was highly involved in what teachers were doing, she had no vision and was not a leader. Laurie explains, "I didn't even know what the word vision was, I just knew there was no connection between what I was doing and what moved the school. There are no school-wide initiatives."

Laurie felt that the principal was content with the status quo and didn't feel the need to focus on student growth because of the school's zip code. The fact that students from affluent communities typically arrive better prepared made Laurie's new school look better than those in many of the surrounding communities where students came from lower socioeconomic neighborhoods. Laurie struggled with the principal's attitude that the school was already very good and that Laurie should not spend time trying to make it better. She questioned why Laurie implemented professional development for the English teachers. The principal asked her, "Why are you doing this? They are already teachers."

Laurie belonged to the school's leadership council, a group which she found to be ironically named because it never shared in any leadership decisions. The principal would bring decisions to council about which she had already made up her mind. It was a place where the principal shared *her* ideas with the group.

Laurie concluded, "At some point, I said, 'I can do more than this. I think I can do her job, and I think that I can bring people together around kids, more student-centered.' I couldn't name all of those things . . . the challenges of multiculturalism, less about race and just more about how you look at the big picture about kids and culture and learning communities."

Laurie left to pursue a doctorate in education with the goal of becoming a secondary school leader. XYZ University was the place where all of those nameless notions of what public education ought to be came together for Laurie. This was the place where Laurie blended theory and practice, putting names to theories and theorists that supported or contradicted her internal compass. Laurie's personal vision was formed through coursework, meaningful preservice experiences, and the opportunity to mentor first-year teachers. Laurie's dissertation ultimately was on teachers' first year of teaching in urban, rural, and suburban settings. At 30 years old, she was ready to take on the challenges of leading a school.

Laurie found that leadership opportunity in a comodel principalship of a high school. It was an exciting time for two 30-year-old women to take on this task for the first time together. The two coprincipals were different in many ways, and Laurie recalls having to quickly define who they were as leaders and what roles each would assume so people could see how they would work together. Laurie considers herself much more community-based, while describing her partner as curriculum-driven. Laurie described that partnership: "I was bringing the theoretical background, and I was bringing all of my PhD work to this, but had never been an assistant principal. She [her coprincipal] was bringing all of her practical work to this. We were meeting, and we worked our butts off!"

Laurie and her coprincipal set the goal of giving voice to kids and to teachers. Their first step was to put teachers in interdisciplinary teams and provide them time to look at data. "We labored over teaming," said Laurie. She and her coprincipal looked at and recognized teachers' strengths and undeveloped strengths and used these to place teachers on teams. Some teachers self-selected, providing reasons why they wanted to work with certain colleagues, while other teachers were purposefully separated by Laurie and her coprincipal.

They reworked the schedule to build in ninth and tenth grade teams with a time set aside each day for the teacher teams to hold common planning or professional learning community time to review student assessments and discuss student needs. More important, Laurie speaks of building in teacher capacity, ensuring that teachers were part of and fully understood the rationale behind each change. One of the keys that Laurie points to as critical to their success was not just lots of strong teacher professional development, but having the coprincipals participate and be seen as fellow learners, participating with the teachers at every professional development event. Through their actions, Laurie and her coprincipal let the teachers know that they were in this together, instead of the all-too-typical leadership mistake of having teachers feel changes were being *done to* them.

Not everyone was receptive to the idea of a new common vision being created for the school. A few staff members wanted to continue to do their own thing; their views were inconsistent with where the vast majority of the school community was headed. Ultimately, those who could not see themselves as a part of what was becoming a new reality for the school—what Laurie refers to as "getting on the bus"—were encouraged to find a school culture that better aligned with their own self-perception.

As teachers found their voice, a common culture began to develop where it was not only acceptable but expected that adults would participate in difficult conversations, giving and receiving hard-to-hear feedback. The adults began to hold each other accountable to their shared vision. When people acted in ways incongruous with shared expectations, they could expect someone to call them on it. Laurie was never shy about holding a mirror up to those she worked with or having a mirror held up to her. Laurie's work was recognized, and she authored the document *High Schools that Work*. After about three years, the district realized they "had a good thing" and asked, "how can we spread it around to the rest of the system?" Laurie was tapped to transform the failing Grades 6–8 middle school.

Laurie stepped into the middle school principalship, promoting the importance of "how do we find the best in each other?" She defined "each other" as not just teachers and administrators, but also as parents, students, and community members. She wrote a grant so that each summer for two weeks the faculty could come together for targeted professional development. The first summer focused on having everyone build a common understanding of middle school philosophy. While teachers could pick components that they wanted to focus on, such as middle school teaming, student advisory, and middle school curriculum, they could not be individual goals but had to benefit the school.

In the second summer, teachers with good ideas were encouraged to find ways to share those ideas with the whole school. The team decided to further examine middle school teaming and how the team could operate similarly while being different. Subsequent summers included professional development on such topics as effectively using rubrics, personalized learning conferences, and standards-based report cards. This summer process of group decision soon became acculturated.

Laurie viewed everyone in the school community as student-learning decision makers. She describes her view of the school community as concentric circles. Students are in the middle, with teachers on the next outer ring, then the broader school community, and in the outermost ring are parents. Each group has a role and ownership for what happens. Laurie views constant clear communication with parents who may not be in the school every day as essential. Constantly communicating what is happening in the school allows the school community to reflect upon school culture and make formative and summative assessments around the culture.

An example of reflecting on school culture was when Laurie led a walk around the school just noticing every sign that read "DON'T." This was eye-opening for the staff as the signs had not been thought about in years; however, once Laurie heightened the staff's awareness of how these signs conveyed underlying messages not conducive to building a learning community, the staff took notice. Soon, more positive and encouraging ways to elicit the desired behavior from students were discovered. Laurie used this activity as a bridge to connect to what needed to happen in the classroom with the use of language conducive to a community of learners.

Laurie feels that one of the lessons she learned was that it takes constant communication on a weekly basis to develop and support teachers as leaders; it cannot be sustained through monthly faculty meetings. "You are waiting for another whole month to bring it back and there are so many gaps that happen." She feels strongly that teacher/principal access to each other as a team is essential, if the principal wants to be an integral part of the team. Group time did not preclude individual teacher and principal time; it was in addition to it. Laurie spent more time in classrooms than in her office. With so much access to the principal, Laurie's faculty meetings were not consumed by a month's worth of unanswered questions and could concentrate on higher order issues.

Another valuable lesson for Laurie was how to handle meetings and information with a careful eye to the distinction between building a personal learning community and a professional learning community, the latter being where people could have those hard conversations with each other. Laurie reflects that without the revolving door of superintendent changes that occurred during her tenure, she may not have been granted the same degree of latitude to share leadership. Laurie recognizes that the locus of control at the school level rests with the principals. Teachers will not be empowered if the superintendent does not empower the principal.

Laurie had always told the staff, "I know I can leave when you know who you want in a leader." Through their time with Laurie, a culture of teacher leadership was fostered and teacher-leaders emerged. When that collection of teacher-leaders could articulate what they wanted in a leader, Laurie knew that her work with them was done.

Case Study Discussion Questions

1. Elaborate on the three most important things Laurie did to change her school(s). What would you do similarly or differently if taking over a failing school?

2. What distinguishes personal learning communities from professional learning communities? Why does understanding the distinction matter?

3. What signs or language choices are taken for granted in your school that should be reexamined?

4. List three ways that your school could improve the clarity and consistency of its communication.

In Summary

Lewis Carroll could have been addressing today's schools when he reflected that until we know where we are going, any road will get us there. Not knowing where we are heading is likely why so many schools can articulate what best practice is but do not actually practice it.

Those who promote the path to personal and professional improvement appear to share a common theme: the importance of beginning with the end in mind. A clear and commonly shared understanding of where the teachers and principal want the school to be in 1, 3, or 5 years will be critical to ending up there. Like the student in Roberta's allegory of the snake, we can easily lose sight of what is important and possibly undermine our efforts.

Even if principals can identify with a high level of specificity the future goal(s) for the school, they cannot get the school there alone. Teachers have the greatest impact on student achievement, but they also cannot get the school to where it needs to be by themselves. Schools have become too complex for principals not to enlist the help of teachers. Those principals who try to go it alone will find that unchecked complexity leads to chaos. To harness the complexity of schools, principals and teachers have to collaborate, each bringing their respective strengths to the partnership. The result is a school culture where teacher-leaders are empowered to share in determining the direction of the school.

Chapter Discussion Questions

In order to not be snake chasers, we need to articulate what is important in our personal and professional lives, determine where we are going, and make plans for how to get there.

1. List the five most important things in your personal life in no particular order.

2. List the five most important things in your professional life in no particular order.

3. Write down your destination. Where do you see yourself in 1 year? In 3 years? In 5 years?

4. List five things that cause you to lose sight of your destination. Complete the sentence: I am a snake chaser when I. . . .

5. Now that you have identified your snakes, come up with a plan for how you will not get lured into chasing them. Complete this sentence: The next time (list one of your specific snakes) bites, I will. . . . Repeat for each of your snakes.

2 A Bountiful Garden

Gardening requires lots of water—most of it in the form of perspiration.

—LOU ERICKSON

I n the same way that a gardener is aware of the conditions conducive to growing a garden (e.g., soil, water, sunshine), the same degree of attention to the conditions in a school are essential for the principal's success in supporting emergent teacher-leaders. A gardener cannot naïvely plant seeds and simply walk away expecting to return at harvest time to find healthy crops; neither can a principal simply identify teacher-leaders and believe that her or his work is done. Creating a teacher-leader-friendly culture is much like tending a garden; without first ensuring a fertile environment and then paying close attention to the growth and development of emergent teacher-leaders, not much can be expected to prosper.

CASE STUDY

Principal Roberta's Story—Continued

The best school leaders find ways to overcome many of the obstacles to creating an environment conducive to appropriate teacher risk-taking. The real question is how and where to begin. Here again we pick up the tale of Principal Roberta when she was appointed as the new principal of Sorrin Elementary School. The Sorrin Elementary School had 550 students in a town wrestling with the growing pains and demographic transformation of moving from a rural to a suburban community. Sorrin Elementary served children from preschool through Grade 6. This was Roberta's second principalship.

Roberta had recently attended a conference of elementary school principals where Mike Schmoker was the keynote speaker. His presentation was entitled *The Opportunity: From "Brutal Facts" to the Best Schools We've Ever Had*. Schmoker used alarming research statistics, "the brutal facts," to demonstrate how, despite volumes of educational studies to the contrary, schools appear wedded to the ineffectual practices of the past that produce mediocre results. Schmoker provided his audience of principals with many concrete strategies for turning their schools around.

Roberta returned to her new school with what she believed was a simple yet highly effective lever to overcome resistance and build momentum. Roberta intuitively knew the power of tackling what Schmoker referred to as "small wins"; she had used that very strategy in addressing faculty concerns identified in her initial needs assessment when she took over the principalship. Yet having one of the current gurus in education tout this approach and support it with research bolstered Roberta's confidence in her approach. She witnessed firsthand how effective celebrating tangible, measureable "small wins" with her faculty was in moving the school forward and impacting the culture. The transformation was not instantaneous, but it was profound.

Every school has "low-hanging fruit," those issues or problems that are relatively easy fixes in regards to time and energy. Roberta had set her sights on addressing those things that the faculty identified as issues before addressing what *she* saw as issues. Roberta openly celebrated each and every small win, stacking them up like souvenirs of where she and her faculty had been. She racked these wins up like trophies of their conquests, and by the middle of year two they had moved up to taking on medium-sized wins, and she had eliminated all but a few small pockets of resistance. Specifics of Roberta's "small win" experiences are explored further in Section Three of this book.

It is worth noting that some teachers and principals are natural skeptics, and that is fine as long as it is a healthy skepticism. Schools do not need everyone onboard to build a culture conducive to fostering teacher-leaders. It is a matter of critical mass. Every weed does not need to be out of the garden to transform culture. If a school's culture is successfully transformed, a time arrives when it will become self-evident to even the most stubborn weed that the collective school culture is about fostering flowers, not weeds. It becomes increasingly uncomfortable to be a weed in a flower garden.

Roberta came to realize that most schools never challenge weeds because they never actually come out and define themselves as flower gardens. Most schools post a mission statement on the wall or print it on the school letterhead, where it sits until the next round of strategic planning or accreditation cycle. How many school mission statements can truly be called living documents? Most mission statements are a colossal waste of time and not lived and breathed by anyone in or out of the school, including the principal. Vague, wholly encompassing mission statements do not change or challenge anyone. The lack of specificity in most mission statements makes it all too easy to remain a weed in the flower garden. Only when school members are very specific, overt, and public about their beliefs will they begin to influence who conducts business in the school and how it is conducted. Roberta knew why so many mission statements just received lip service: challenging the status quo is difficult, uncomfortable, and potentially job threatening for a new principal. Roberta had a graduate school professor who used to say, "People like change, but they don't want to be changed."

Roberta thought to herself, "How many teachers, students, or parents in our school could recite our school's mission statement?" If the mission statement identifies the reasons we do what we do, why are so few mission statements a part of the educational conversations in schools? When was the last time a teacher said, "Hey, let's consult our mission statement to help guide us in our decision making?" A mission statement is typically a vague, "feel-good" notion incapable of being a guiding compass. If a school is going to create a common mission and publicly display it for the world to see, then it needs to be a clear, concise compact to which the school faculty agrees to hold each other.

FINDING COMMON GROUND

Mission statements usually include the most current buzz phrases, such as "We strive to help our students become lifelong learners." The groups that come up with mission statements usually stop well short of the difficult work of challenging themselves. A mission statement that represents the least common denominator challenges no one. Schools end up with a nebulous notion that no two people define the same way. Anyone walking into a classroom would not be able to parse out which activities were in line with the school's mission and which were not. These statements encompass almost everybody, challenge nobody, and are why so many schools are like poorly pruned gardens.

The members of any organization, not just schools, need to be willing to have uncomfortable conversations; they need to establish a common understanding of what their organization does and does not stand for. Ideally the mission of an organization should cause its members to measure the alignment of their personal missions and, through doing so, develop a deeper understanding of what being a part of that organization really means. Publicly and specifically identifying what we stand for both collectively and individually is uncomfortable, which is why so few schools take on this task in earnest. Done well, building a collective mission statement would require members of the organization to face individual beliefs contrary to the organization.

Organizations could take collective beliefs to the extreme by too narrowly defining collective beliefs; differing opinions make an organization stronger. Too narrowly or too broadly defining organizational beliefs is a disservice. The shared core beliefs of the school are the basic tenets that should guide what is done, why it is done, and how it is done. If a teacher candidate applying for a position were to ask any member of the school "What does this school believe?," each member should be able to articulate a "We believe . . ." statement. Those candidates whose *core* beliefs were not aligned with the school's should seek employment elsewhere. It is okay to have a few daisies in a rose garden, but not radishes. Those whose beliefs are contrary to the common mission of the school will be miserable and make everyone around them miserable. Even new teachers who share core beliefs with the school should be part of a robust new teacher induction and mentoring program. It is essential that prospective principals find a good match when looking for a potential school. A principal whose core values are not aligned with the school community's core values will not likely be very successful. As a prospective principal or teacher, telling interview committees what you think they want to hear may be a strategy that brings immediate satisfaction; however, taking on a new job ought to be viewed as a long-term commitment.

CELEBRATING WINS

What does it mean to "celebrate" wins? Some examples include announcing wins in the school newsletter, sharing wins at school committee meetings, sharing wins at PTO meetings, sending individual or group emails recognizing wins and praising those who helped to accomplish the wins, and giving a shout out at faculty meetings. In other words, taking any opportunity or venue to recognize building momentum toward positive change. A couple of caveats need to be mentioned about small wins. The principal has to be sincere in recognizing genuine wins; he or she cannot under any circumstances manufacture wins or provide false praise. In the beginning, the principal should be cautious and only tackle wins that he or she is confident can be won; there will be time later on for risk taking.

This action is not simply about celebrating small wins and patting each other on the back. It is about building momentum in order to position the school community to successfully take on big wins. It is about creating a collective attitude and changing the school community's self-perception.

PRINCIPAL PARADIGM SHIFTING

Schools are not places for megalomaniacs. To bring about change, administrators have to leave their egos at the door. This sounds easier to accomplish than it actually is. As the saying goes, denial is not just a river in Egypt. Every principal reading this is saying, "Who, me?" To that we say, "Yes, you!"

Educators strive to become administrators for a variety of reasons, most of which are altruistic. Whether we wish to admit it or not, the majority of principals cannot help but identify themselves with their jobs. Over time, a principal's sense of self-worth becomes entwined with how he or she perceives how others perceive his or her effectiveness as a school leader.

Identifying herself with her position is not unique to Roberta the principal or to any of us. School administrators share the propensity for this trait with people in all walks of life. It is human nature to associate oneself with one's chosen occupation. We often feel that we are what we do. The next time you are introduced to someone, pay attention to the next question your new acquaintance asks after learning your name. More likely than not you will be asked, "What do you do?" You probably will not answer that you are a great husband or wife, a loving father or mother, or a passionate gardener, or that you make a mean meatloaf, or that you line dance every Thursday night at the Elks hall. Ask someone what they "do" and they will no doubt reply by telling you about their job: "I am a stockbroker," "I am a nurse," "I am a police officer," "I am a letter carrier," "I own the local hardware store," and the list goes on and on. We all know people who have struggled with retirement because their sense of identity was so tied up in their occupation that they seemed to flounder once they lost that sense of purpose.

A principal not being able to separate self from job will stand in the way, often unwittingly, of supporting teacher-leaders. In the last chapter of this text, on building sustainability, we will further explore the importance for principals to define themselves more broadly than just through their profession, and pursue out-of-school interests, fulfilling them in ways that can recharge their batteries.

Principals worry about abdicating authority and losing power by sharing what they identify as their job—school leadership—with teachers. Identifying so strongly with our roles makes giving up some of what has traditionally been our bailiwick tantamount to letting go of a piece of our identity. We state in the kindest possible way that in order to bring about cultural change, administrators must check their egos at the door.

Here are the cold, hard facts supported by decades of research. While principals are important, teachers are the number one factor in impacting student achievement. The teachers are the MVPs of the school. This may be difficult for some administrators to accept, but it is teachers who hold the key to school change. Before every principal reading this book decides it would be best utilized under the leg of the patio table to prevent that irksome wobble, please hear this again—*principals are important*! Principals just need a slight paradigm shift in their thinking.

Louis, Leithwood, Wahlstrom, and Anderson (2010) revisited their original claim about the importance of principals at the onset of a 6-year study. They found, "based on a preliminary review of research, that leadership is second only to classroom instruction as an influence on student learning, after six additional years of research, we are even more confident about this claim" (p. 9).

Principals' influence is secondary to that of teachers because principals' influence on students is indirect while teachers' influence is direct; but principals' influence on *teachers* is direct. Wahlstrom and Louis (2008) have concisely captured the principal issue: "in the current era of accountability, a principal's responsibility for the quality of teachers' work is simply a fact of life. How to achieve influence over work settings (classrooms) in which they rarely participate is a key dilemma" (p. 459).

Sebastian and Allensworth (2012) speak to the indirect power of principals to impact student achievement. They suggest that intuitively it makes sense that the leadership of principals "has the greatest association with the overall quality of instruction and student achievement through the school learning climate. School climate affects all classrooms and so may have the broadest reach across the many different classes in a school" (p. 20).

Heifetz (1994) frames leadership as an activity more than a position. Heifitz further distinguishes leadership problems as either "technical" problems or "adaptive" problems. The ability to recognize the distinction between management problems and leadership problems is key to changing school culture. Some principals possess impressive skills that make them fabulous managers, but terrible leaders.

THE SILENT CONDUCTOR

A few years ago, Benjamin Zander addressed a group of school principals. The topic was the Art of Possibility, which was also the title of a book that he coauthored with his wife Rosamund Stone Zander (2000). Rosamund is a family systems therapist and an executive coach, and Benjamin is the conductor of the Boston Philharmonic. There is a section in their book entitled *Leading from Any Chair*. Maestro Zander writes:

> I had been conducting for nearly twenty years when it suddenly dawned on me that the conductor of an orchestra does not make a sound. His picture may appear on the cover of the CD in various dramatic poses, but his true power derives from his ability to make other people powerful. I began to ask myself questions like "What makes a group of people lively and engaged?" instead of "how good am I?" So palpable was the difference in my approach to conducting as a result of this "silent conductor" insight, that players in the orchestra started asking me, "What happened to you?" Before that, my main concerns had been whether the audience was appreciating my

interpretation and, if the truth were known, whether the critics like it because if they did it might lead to other opportunities and greater success. In order to realize my interpretation of the work in question, it seemed all I had to do was to gain sway over the players, teach them my interpretation, and make them fulfill my musical will. Now in the light of my "discovery," I began to shift my attention to how effective I was at enabling the musicians to play each phrase as beautifully as they were capable. This concern had rarely surfaced when my position appeared to give me absolute power and I had cast the players as mere instruments of my will. (pp. 68–69)

Maestro Zander phrases it this way: "How much greatness are we willing to grant?" (p. 73). Describing the role of the leader this way places the onus squarely on the leader's shoulders. In the case of school principals, the question may be rephrased as "How much leadership are you willing to allow teachers?"

VANTAGE POINT AND PERSPECTIVE

School principals are to symphony conductors as teachers are to members of the orchestra. Much depends upon the conductor's ability to elicit the full potential out of the musicians with whom he or she works but, as Maestro Zander points out, at the end of the concert the conductor hasn't played a single note. The difference for the orchestra member, or the classroom teacher, is a matter of perspective. The conductor and the principal have a big-picture perspective. The orchestra conductor gains a vantage point by standing on the rostrum. Before the age of military satellites and unmanned surveillance drones, field marshals and generals would position themselves on the hills overlooking the battlefield, not because they were cowards, but because it provided a better vantage point, affording them the best perspective with which to lead their troops. Principals do not stand on a rostrum or climb to the top of the nearest hill; instead, they gain a whole-school vantage point through situational awareness.

As noted in chapter one, Marzano, Waters, and McNulty (2005) performed a meta-analysis on the relationship between principals' responsibilities and students' achievement. It was found that the strongest correlation between principal responsibilities and student achievement centered on a principal's situational awareness. Put another way, principals with the best perspective of what was happening in their school had the greatest impact on student achievement.

Situational awareness of the whole school is a vantage point that most classroom teachers are not in a position to possess due to the traditional structure in most schools, which presents a paradox. Principals possess the vantage point while teachers are the number one factor in student achievement. This book is about breaking out of the very traditional top-down hierarchical model in the majority of schools and fostering real teacher leadership.

It is essential for principals to guide emergent teacher-leaders who may not yet have gained a school-wide vantage point. When Roberta was a young girl, her elderly grandmother had the Serenity Prayer hanging up in her kitchen. Every reader has no doubt encountered some variation of this petition:

God grant me the serenity to accept the things I cannot change,

Courage to change the things I can,

And wisdom to know the difference

This notion of the "wisdom to know the difference" between the things that can and cannot be changed, and by whom, is particularly critical for school leaders to understand. The prayer does not mention "when," but effective leaders understand the importance of timing. There is a time to bolster up one's courage and change the things that they can and a time when discretion is the rule of the day.

BUILDING COLLECTIVE EFFICACY

Wahlstrom and Louis (2008) recognize the concept of collective sense of responsibility. "Principals, who step beyond merely managing, emphasize the construction of cultures where teachers' believe that they not only have the capacity to influence student learning but the shared obligation to do so. Collective responsibility is often regarded as the outcome of collective efficacy" (p. 466). Goddard and Goddard (2001) discovered that the efficacy of individual teachers was higher in the schools where the collective efficacy of teachers was higher.

Trust in the principal is not enough. In their study, Wahlstrom and Louis found their initial assumption that trust makes up many of the paving stones on the path to improving instructional practices and ultimately leads to improved student learning was not as significant as originally thought. They suspect this is "because trust in the principal by the teacher is often a diffuse element of the school's environment" (p. 482). They go on to explain that "the principal may be perceived as caring about and supportive of good instruction but may still not have much to say about the deliberate strategic choices that teachers make when designing or changing classroom practice" (p. 482).

NOT SOWING MORE THAN YOU CAN REAP

It can be demoralizing for both teacher and principal when the budding teacher-leader feels empowered to take those first tentative steps outside of their comfort zone and take on change, only to discover that the change was outside of their sphere of influence or their timing was off. Through experience, the leader of leaders learns to discern between what is within and what is without the influential sphere for each role in the school, including her or his own.

The line of demarcation between the sphere of concern and sphere of influence is not etched in stone; this line is unique to each school, and will expand for the emergent teacher-leaders to encompass a greater sphere of influence as the roles of teacher-leader and principal evolve within the culture of the school (see Figure 2.1).

BUILDING CAPACITY

The whole teacher-leader movement is about building the capacity of schools to better serve students. Waldron and McLeskey (2010) define school capacity as "the infrastructure and resources available within a school to address student needs. Capacity includes concrete and tangible elements such as finances, personnel, and scheduling as well as intangible elements such as school climate and vision" (p. 69). Fullan (2006) emphasizes, "collaborative cultures are ones that focus on building the capacity for continuous improvement and are intended to be a new way of working and learning. They are meant to be enduring capacities, not just another program innovation" (p. 10).

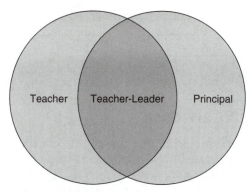

FIGURE 2.1 Overlapping roles of teacher, teacher-leader, and principal.

The demands and complexity of the modern school have outstripped the leadership capacity of any one person. The days of principals acting alone to manage all but the tiniest schools are gone. The most effective principals are the ones enlisting the help of others. Principals now reside in an era of collaborative leadership. Hallinger and Heck (2010) suggest, "collaborative leadership focuses on strategic school-wide actions that are directed towards school improvement and shared among the principal, teachers, administrators, and others" (p. 97). In their empirical study over a period of four years, Hallinger and Heck assessed the effects of collaborative leadership on school improvement capacity and student learning using a large sample of primary schools in the United States. They described collaborative leadership as entailing "the use of governance structures and organizational processes that empowered staff and students, encouraged broad participation in decision-making, and fostered shared accountability for student learning" (p. 97).

COMMON FINDINGS EMERGE FROM TEACHER-LEADER RESEARCH

There appear to be themes in the suggested findings from teacher-leader research over the past few decades. Louis, Leithwood, Wahlstrom, and Anderson (2010) defined collective leadership in their research findings as the term used to refer to the "extent of influence that organizational members and stakeholders exert on decisions in their schools" (p. 19). This narrow perspective on leadership of leadership as influence was selected for its focus on the combined effects of all sources of leadership and recognition that there are potential differences in the contributions made by different groups of stakeholders (i.e., principals, teachers, students, and parents).

Louis et al. list the following as key findings of *Collective Leadership Effects on Teachers and Students*:

- Collective leadership has a stronger influence on student achievement than individual leadership.
- Almost all people associated with high-performing schools have greater influence on school decisions than is the case with people in low-performing schools.
- Higher-performing schools award greater influence to teacher teams, parents, and students, in particular.

- Principals and district leaders have the most influence on decisions in all schools; however, they do not lose influence as others gain influence.
- School leaders have an impact on student achievement primarily through their influence on teachers' motivation and working conditions; their influence on teachers' knowledge and skills produces less impact on student achievement.

Berg et al. (2005) studied second-stage teachers and why they take on teacher leadership positions. They used the term "second-stage teacher" to describe those teachers who are still relatively new to the profession yet have "achieved tenure and a sense of confidence about their classroom teaching, these teachers are in the second stage of their careers" (p. 4). This period was characterized as the decade after obtaining tenure. Berg et al. found that in taking on and performing teacher-leader roles, second-stage teachers "wanted, above all, to make a difference beyond their classrooms" (p. 5). "Making a difference" was construed to mean different things for different teacher-leaders. It included "influencing how teachers interact with one another and teach their classes, to changing how students experience school, to shaping policies that, in turn, affect the structure of schools" (p. 25). The desire of teachers to make a difference—their driving motivation—cannot be underrated. Leithwood and Mascall (2008) found the strongest link between the influence of collective leadership and student achievement to be teachers' motivation.

Berg et al. found that principals who possess a vision for how teacher-leaders will be integrated into the school's academic goals for the future should openly communicate the purpose of teacher-leaders and articulate the value teacher-leaders bring to the school. Through actively clarifying what will be required to achieve the school's goals and precisely how the role of teacher-leaders fits into that plan, ambiguity is eliminated. One of the participants in the study termed this necessity of a concise principal vision the "big game plan." Another participant called her principal the "green light guy" who approved her proposals, but did not inspire the school with a shared vision for the future. Passive support of teacher-leaders by the principal is not sufficient to create a shared vision for school improvement. The successful recipe calls for articulated vision, principal support, and inspiration.

"Structural supports that are in place school-wide allow teachers in [leadership] roles to have easy access to their colleagues" (p. 27). Examples of these structures included well-structured and purposeful staff meetings, professional development opportunities that are sustained, and common planning time to discuss teaching practices. The authors of the study offered a note of caution about the importance of maintaining consistency in leadership, even when principal turnover occurs. They suggest, "mechanisms must be put in place to ensure the maintenance of a strong vision for the school, as well as roles linked to that vision" (p. 27). Sustainable distributive leadership ensures an enduring vision despite changes in the principalship.

Weiner (2011) published a study that investigated the experiences of a small group of teacher-leaders and their principals. Weiner suggests five key insights from her study that can better help those trying to understand the relationship between principals and teacher leadership.

1. ***Clear Vision and Inclusive Process***—Teacher leadership must be a part of the clear vision of school reform that the principal creates. This process needs to be collaborative and include training and support, which involves the principals, teacher-leaders, and the broader school community.

2. ***Training***—All teacher-leaders must clearly understand and be knowledgeable about the skills necessary to implement their roles. Principals too must be taught how to create a transparent process to identify, select, and foster teacher-leaders.

3. ***Allocate Resources***—Principals must consider both their own and the teacher-leaders' schedules, workloads, and time commitments to ensure that teacher-leaders are positioned for success with time for principals to effectively support teacher-leaders. Principals must also encumber sufficient funding to support and carry out any staffing changes.

4. ***Overcoming School Norms***—Schools can be extremely egalitarian. Traditional school norms can make it difficult to recruit teacher-leaders and for established teacher-leaders to find support among the faculty. Principals need familiarity [situational awareness] about the school's norms in order to effectively stem resistance to teacher leadership.

5. ***Overcoming Do It Yourself-ism*** —Teacher-leaders often resort to "doing it themselves" rather than confronting the resistance of other teachers. Weiner found that while this action "tended to diminish teacher resistance," it simultaneously diminished teacher-leaders' effectiveness. Teacher-leaders require a close partnership with their principal, who must become better prepared to support emergent teacher-leaders to overcome resistance and change norms.

Knight (2009) addressed the question "What can we do about teacher resistance?" in an article by the same name. Knight posed that a more appropriate question might be "What can we do to make it easier for teachers to implement new practices? (p. 508). He suggests that "teacher resistance" can stem from a multitude of issues. In particular, the previous experiences of teachers influence their level of resistance.

When coaching change leaders, Knight uses the short documentary *The Waters of Ayole* to drive home the point that experience trumps talk every time.

The short film describes the efforts of United Nations aid workers to support villages as they take care of village water pumps, literally a matter of life or death for many villagers. In the scene, four village leaders are asked what they thought when they learned they were getting a pump for their village. "At first, we weren't particularly pleased," they say. "We thought it might be a trick. And people refused to come to meetings. When the machines arrived . . . we were afraid they might scare us away from our village. Without seeing the water, we weren't convinced. Even when the water gushed out, without having drunk any of it, we still weren't convinced." What finally convinced the villagers? "The day water came from the pump and we drank it. Then we said these people really did something for us." Even when offered something that is lifesaving, people may resist until they actually experience the phenomenon (p. 510).

Knight's experience has been, "When it comes to change, teachers have to drink the water, so to speak, before they will believe" (p. 510).

York-Barr and Duke (2004), in their study of two decades of teacher leadership, also found too much ambiguity in the roles of teacher-leaders. Their study suggested that the "likelihood of being successful as a teacher-leader is increased if roles and expectations are mutually shaped and negotiated by teacher-leaders, their colleagues, and principals on the basis of context-specific (and changing) instructional and improvement needs" (p. 288).

York-Barr and Duke believe principals play a pivotal role in the success of teacher-leadership. They defined teacher-leadership as "the process by which teachers, individually or collectively, influence their colleagues, principals, and other members of school communities to improve teaching and learning practices with the aim of increased student learning and achievement" (p. 288). Their findings point to the primary means by which teacher-leaders influence other teachers: through constructing collaborative relationships based on trust. Principals can take on the role of "actively supporting the development of teachers, by maintaining open channels of communication, and by aligning structures and resources to support the leadership work of teachers" (p. 288), yet those structures were found to be severely lacking.

In Summary

Principals and the principalship matter; principals' impact on student learning is second only to teachers' impact on student learning. Principals are critical to the success of a school, but it is unrealistic to hold them up as some kind of superhuman. Principals have to separate themselves from their titles; it will take a collaborative effort to transform a school's culture and see a bountiful garden through to fruition.

Being a passive supporter or simply a trusted administrator is not enough for modern-day principals. Over the last 50 years, schools have become increasingly complex entities. In order to effectively harness the complexity of the modern school, principals will have to work collaboratively to create a clear and concise vision for where the school is heading. If this includes revisiting the school's mission plan, then the mission plan cannot be an all-encompassing, meaningless document, nor can it be so narrowly construed as to not profess the commonly held beliefs of the school community. Any vision to be collaboratively held should be collaboratively created to include all stakeholders, and has to specifically outline the roles of teacher-leaders. The teacher-leaders' place in the school-wide vision has to be supported with structural and financial resources.

Expect teacher-leaders to encounter resistance from their colleagues; building collective efficacy takes time and much preparation. Principal Roberta began racking up "small wins" by addressing the easy fixes, sure wins, and low-hanging fruit. She never falsified results by trying to make wins that were not there and never offered false praise. She did celebrate wins, giving credit where credit was due. It took Roberta 2½ years to build the momentum to be in a position to take on the bigger challenges.

Once a commonly shared vision is in place, it is time to ensure succession planning. Ask the question, "How will teacher-leaders and their contributions be supported if the principal leaves?" Teacher leadership needs to be systemic. In short, the future of the school's vision cannot rest with one person.

Chapter Discussion Questions

1. Was Roberta correct to address those things that the faculty identified as issues before addressing what she saw as issues? Support your answer.
2. Make a short list of the things you can and cannot change in your school. If you cannot change them, who can?
3. How does Maestro Zander's "silent conductor" theory apply to school leaders? How much greatness are you willing to grant? What would make the group of people you work with lively and engaged?
4. Who are the emergent teacher-leaders in your school? What roles do they fulfill?

3

A Leader of Leaders

As we look ahead into the next century, leaders will be those who empower others.

—BILL GATES

SHIFTING THE PRINCIPAL'S ROLE FROM "LEADER" TO "LEADER OF LEADERS"

This chapter is about principals using a new frame to view their role. In this new frame, "teachers are the primary instructional decision makers in the school. The principal is not seen as the sole instructional leader but rather as the leader of instructional leaders" (Glickman, 1989, p. 6). In this model, teacher-leaders become the principal's partners.

When decision making becomes distributed, teacher-leaders are empowered and supported. It stands to reason that when teachers are involved in shared decision making they will be more inclined to have greater participation, share their views, and offer more efficient alternatives. "Distributed leadership concentrates on engaging expertise wherever it exists within the organization rather than seeking this only through formal position or role" (Harris & Muijs, 2005, p. 25). Teachers are often in a better position than principals to understand what is not working in a school.

Cultivating teacher leadership for enhanced school performance is essential to school improvement (Marks & Printy, 2003). Marks and Printy's integrated view of leadership found that "to enlarge the leadership capacity of schools attempting to improve their academic performance, some principals involve teachers in sustained dialogue and decision making about educational matters" (p. 370). Those principals that enlist teachers in shared leadership decisions discover that teachers possess both the desire and the expertise to lead. When this occurs, there is a "synergistic power of leadership shared by individuals throughout the school" (p. 393).

This change in culture positively impacts school improvement or, put another way, "School improvement is essentially a process of changing school culture. To achieve this, teachers need to be committed to a process of change that involves them in examining and changing their own practice" (Harris & Lambert, 2003, p. 14).

Marks and Printy found that neither instructional leadership—the top-down, principal-in-charge type of leadership—nor transformational leadership—where the principal provides the "intellectual direction and aims at innovating within the organization" (p. 371)—were sufficient to bring about school improvement. They suggest that a hybrid of the two leadership styles *does* bring about substantial results in quality of instruction and student achievement. Shared leadership involves "the active collaboration of principal and teachers on curriculum, instruction, and assessment" (p. 371).

Marks and Printy have "reconceptualized" the meaning of instructional leadership to incorporate a more innovative approach that abandons the old hierarchical model and replaces it with "shared instructional leadership." Shared instructional leadership necessitates that a principal adapts her or his role to one that actively seeks out the "ideas, insights, and expertise of teachers in these areas and works with teachers for school improvement. The principal and teachers share responsibility for staff development, curricular development, and supervision of instructional tasks" (p. 371).

PARADIGM SHIFTING

There is a pivotal scene in the film *The Milagro Beanfield War* (warning: spoiler alert) that serves as a wonderful analogy for the power of the paradigm shift a school culture undergoes when teachers are transformed into teacher-leaders. *The Milagro Beanfield War* is a Sundance film directed by Robert Redford in 1988. It weaves the tale of a rural farming community with a population of fewer than 500 people somewhere in the American Southwest. The protagonist, Joe Mondragon, is a poor farmer who refuses to sell out to the politically connected big business interests with plans to develop the area. The development will provide the short-term benefits of construction jobs, but ultimately destroy the farming community. As part of the plan, local farms are legally, albeit unethically, being starved of the life-giving water necessary to irrigate their fields. Joe begins diverting water from a pipe that runs across his bean field, which is destined for use in the nearby development project.

The tension builds when the townspeople helplessly stand by as state authorities come to Joe's field to take him into custody. There appears to be nothing local sheriff Bernie Montoya can do, despite his sympathies for the farmers, as agents sent by the governor wade into the crowd to apprehend Joe. All seems lost when Sheriff Montoya suddenly announces to the crowd that he is deputizing all of them and ordering them to protect Joe. In an instant, a profound paradigm shift occurs. The handful of state agents are suddenly surrounded not by a group of helpless townspeople but by a band of sworn sheriff's deputies intent on protecting Joe.

When a school's official leader "deputizes" the teachers to fulfill the mission of the school, a powerful paradigm shift occurs in which teachers go from bystanders in a traditional system with a hierarchical top-down style of management to active participants charged with leading their schools. Just as Sheriff Montoya was not alone in facing the struggles of his office, neither are principals alone in facing the struggles of their office. Principals cannot find success without deputizing others committed to a common cause.

THE JOURNEY

We are, each one of us, the culmination of our collective experiences. Those who become the leaders of leaders find that no previous experience was wasted. Every endeavor carries with it some valuable takeaway; even the smallest nugget may someday serve to solve a problem, improve a process, or simply create a better understanding of where another person is coming from.

John Steinbeck (1980), in *Travels with Charley: In Search of America*, described how his exploration differed from other journeys: "A trip, a safari, an exploration, is an entity, different from all other journeys. It has personality, temperament, individuality, and uniqueness. A journey is a person in itself; no two are alike" (p. 3).

Each school leader's journey is also unique, as is each school's transformation from point A, the status quo, to point B, the desirable future. Each possesses a personality, temperament, individuality, and uniqueness. No two transformations are identical. Even transformations in the same building, separated by several years, will be completely unique unto themselves. The school is never in exactly the same place from one year to the next: teachers retire, new teachers are hired, principals move on, different members are elected to the school board, the economy changes, the flavor of the town or city shifts in one direction or another, and the list goes on.

PRINCIPAL ROBERTA'S JOURNEY TO LEADERSHIP

Before becoming a school administrator, Principal Roberta found herself working in what turned out to be a transitional job from the end of the '80s and into the mid-'90s. Little did she know at the time that what she viewed as her "between careers" job would end up having such a profound impact on her thinking as a school leader decades into the future.

She had dabbled in law enforcement for 5 years. No doubt thousands of sheriff's deputies and police officers across the country find that a sense of contribution is the very thing that keeps them pinning on the badge each day, but while Roberta appreciated the contributions lawmen bring to society, the occupation never satiated her thirst to make a difference.

She had just called it quits with her venture into police work in the spring of 1989 when her best friend suggested that she apply to work with her at a soap manufacturing plant on the outskirts of a major urban center. Her friend argued that while Roberta was undecided about what to do next, factory work would pay relatively well; and besides, what did she have to lose by working at the soap plant for a year while she weighed her options? The year of weighing her options turned into 5 years.

Roberta is still struck by how what she initially saw as the monotonous job of watching soap whiz past on a conveyor line was actually filled with richly rewarding trainings and experiences that have had a profound influence in shaping her subsequent thinking about organizational leadership. This was during a time just prior to the ratification of the North American Free Trade Agreement (NAFTA) in 1994, at the height of the influence of giants in organizational and managerial thinking. The influence of organizational thinkers like Peter Drucker, W. Edward Demming, and Peter Senge on American manufacturing was huge.

The better part of her time within manufacturing was spent exploring, perfecting, and piloting High-Performing Work Systems (HPWS). The company supported and even encouraged her experiments with HPWS, which was a deviation from the traditional employer-employee model. Employees in HPWS had greater autonomy, but in exchange they accepted greater ownership.

You may be asking yourself, what does working in a soap factory have to do with educational leadership in the second decade of the 21st century? It wasn't until Roberta became a school principal that she even began to see the connection. None of her life's experiences were truly wasted. So much of what Roberta holds true about the power of teacher-leaders blossomed from seeds sown working to create HPWS in the manufacturing environment.

Those developing a culture to support teacher-leaders may find that High Performing Work Systems theory and history will provide a solid foundation to empower those who do not hold official leadership titles (see Appendix A).

THE LEADER'S ROLE IN BUILDING A TEAM

Leadership needs to be broader than just the principal; ". . . the key notion in this definition of leadership is that leadership is about learning together and constructing meaning and knowledge collectively and collaboratively" (Harris & Lambert, 2003, p. 16), and the key to creating enduring, positive, and high performing changes in organization culture resides in five crucial conditions (Juechter, Fisher, & Alford, 1998). They describe culture change as an "intense, complex process . . . [that] takes time and challenges people to call on the best in themselves and others to see beyond that complexity and achieve results" (p. 66).

The five crucial conditions are:

1. A relevant focus
2. Driven from the top, but fueled throughout the organization
3. Leaders' commitment
4. Comprehensive involvement
5. External coaches

A relevant focus refers to tying changes to real-life situations. Driven from the top, but fueled throughout the organization means that the principal can lead the change, but cannot "fuel" the change. "Its [that change is organization-wide] importance cannot be overstated. Senior leaders must be part of the change, must experience the change . . ." (p. 66). The leader has to "commit to a systemic, organization-wide approach to cultural change" (p. 66). Juechter et al. drive home the importance of comprehensive involvement through a rather tongue-in-cheek memo, which reads:

"Dear Valued Employee:
The following contains a list of new values
agreed upon by senior management in our recent
retreat. Please implement them immediately . . ." (p. 66).

Meaningful change will not be *done to* the teachers; it must be *made with* the teachers. The final condition is to use external coaches because everyone in the organization is too close to put things in perspective objectively.

The leaders of leaders will lead not simply a group of teacher-leaders, but a *team* of teacher-leaders. The distinction between a *group* of individuals working toward a common goal (a working group) and a *team* of individuals working toward a common goal is significant. Before exploring some of the relevant thinking from High Performance Work Systems that applies to principals and teachers, it is worth noting how teams are distinguished from working groups.

Katzenbach and Smith (2005) offer the following distinction between working groups and teams. Working groups have a strong, clearly focused leader, while teams share leadership roles. In working groups individuals are accountable, while in teams there exists both individual and mutual accountability. The group's purpose is the same as the organizational mission in working groups, yet teams can have a specific team purpose that drives the team itself. Working groups produce individual work-products; teams produce collective work-products. Working groups run efficient meetings while teams encourage open-ended discussion and active problem solving at meetings. Effectiveness is measured indirectly by the influence of others in working groups, but effectiveness in teams is a performance measure directly assessing collective work products. Working groups discuss, decide, and delegate; teams discuss, decide, and do real work together.

Teams hold each other accountable and are able to have difficult conversations. Van Knippenberg, De Dreu, and Homan (2004) speak to the need for teams to go through the process of reconciling conflicting viewpoints. The objective is to force a group "to more thoroughly process task-relevant information and may prevent the group from opting too easily for a course of action on which there seems to be consensus" (p. 1009). Van den Bossche, Gijselaers, Segers, Woltjer and Kirschner (2010) have done a concise job of paraphrasing van Knippenberg et al. in demonstrating that conflict, as long as it is constructive, is the path to reaching a shared mental model. The role of constructive conflict is critical. This occurs by taking a critical stance regarding each other's contributions, and by considering each other's comments and ideas. Only when each team member can "address differences in opinion and can speak freely, will there really be construction of a shared mental model. If this behavior is lacking, team learning is not taking place" (p. 296).

Mental models are a reoccurring theme in leading a team. Mental models as described by Norman (1983) are naturally evolving models where people's view of themselves, their capacities, and the world around them strongly influence how they approach tasks that they are asked to perform or topics they are asked to learn. Norman speaks about how one's conceptualization of self, others, and the world influence what he or she brings to each task: "In interacting with the environment, with others, and with the artifacts of technology, people form internal, mental models of themselves and of the things with which they are interacting" (p. 7). Senge (1990) defines mental models as "deeply ingrained assumptions, generalizations, or even pictures and images that influence how we understand the world and how we take action" (p. 8). Senge speaks of mental models as the opportunity for "learningful" conversations where "people expose their own thinking effectively and make that thinking open to the influence of others" (p. 9).

One of the main tasks for the leader is to have the thinking of individual team members be open to the influence of others. Opening up the thinking of individuals is essential to building a collective shared mental model for what it means to be a member of the team, and ultimately leads to a shared vision organizationally for where the school is headed. Before individuals expose their personal mental model to others, a culture of trust and acceptance needs to pervade the team.

Salas, Sims, and Burke (2005) outline the "big five" in teamwork as:

1. Team leadership
2. Mutual performance monitoring
3. Backup behavior
4. Adaptability
5. Team orientation

In this chapter, our focus is on team leadership. Salas et al. identify three overarching functions for the team leader:

1. Create and maintain the team's mental model.
2. Facilitate team effectiveness and adaptability. Monitor the internal and external environment of the team. "Ensure teams are not caught off guard when changes in their environment occur" (p. 573). Promote team effectiveness by "using the information about the external environment. Coordinate team behaviors and interactions. Provide skill development opportunities as needed" (p. 573).
3. Establish expectations for acceptable interaction patterns as well as behavioral and performance expectations. Track team member abilities and skill deficiencies. "Create a team climate that encourages behaviors such as mutual performance monitoring, backup behavior, and adaptability. Developing task-based and team-based norms benefits teams because individual members will enforce norms and team expectations in nonconforming members" (p. 573).

Let's stop for a moment to define what is meant by "backup behavior." Marks, Mathieu, and Zaccaro (2000) describe backup behavior in teams as:

1. Providing a teammate verbal feedback behavior or coaching
2. Helping a teammate behaviorally in carrying out actions
3. Assuming and completing a task for a teammate (p. 363)

Backup behavior is one of the teacher team commitments that Park, Henkin, and Egley (2005) list. Teacher team members commit to backup behavior when they:

1. Fill in for another member who is unable to perform a task.
2. Seek opportunities to aid other team members.
3. Provide assistance to those who need it.

LEADERS CREATE OPERATING CULTURES THAT ENCOURAGE A SENSE OF TRUST

Leaders create operating cultures that encourage a sense trust, of being in this together. This causes those working with the leader to feel comfortable with appropriate risk taking. For emergent teacher-leaders, this type of culture is essential to their sustained success. Hoffman, Bynum, Piccolo, and Sutton (2011) discovered that "if a leader's values and those of his/her organization are not aligned, mixed messages result and can leave organizational members confused about their roles or disillusioned with their organization" (p. 791).

Dr. Randy Pausch was a Carnegie Mellon professor who, on September 18, 2007, delivered a talk billed as the "last lecture" (Pausch, 2008). Randy had been diagnosed with terminal cancer and this was an opportunity for him to share some final thoughts and beliefs with the world, and especially with his children. In his lecture, Randy told the story of an incredible opportunity presented to him to take a leave of absence from his university post to fulfill the lifelong ambition of collaborating with the Disney Company. Imbedded in his story, he offered a lesson for every leader.

Randy approached his first boss and told him of this incredible opportunity, and his boss could only see all of the brick walls—every reason why it couldn't work. Randy went higher up the chain to the next boss; while this leader could not see how it would work, he remained open to exploring the possibility. Randy told his audience, "They both said [each boss] the same thing [that they did not know how this was going to work]. But think about how they said it, right? . . . They're both ways of saying 'I don't know,' but boy there's a good way and a bad way." The second boss saw a well-respected faculty member excited about an opportunity, so he was willing to listen. He validated Randy as an employee and gave credence to, though not necessarily acceptance of, Randy's idea.

Randy ultimately got to work in collaboration with Disney because his second boss did not close the door to possibility, and because Randy believed that "brick walls are there to give us a chance to show how badly we want something. Because the brick walls are there to stop the people who don't want it badly enough. They're there to stop the other people" (p. 52). Randy succumbed to cancer in 2008.

Dr. Chris McCusker served for a decade as a faculty member at Yale University's School of Management and is now a senior consultant at Turknett Leadership Group in Atlanta. McCusker describes four key challenges for any leadership team hoping to change an organization's operating culture. McCusker (2004) describes operating culture as "the way we do things around here" (p. 1). McCusker's four key challenges for organizational change are:

1. Evaluate the status quo—Leaders determine if and why change is necessary. This is done by diagnosing the status quo to assemble evidence in support of the change. McCusker points out that this process begins with examining the leader's own role in the change.
2. Articulate a vision—Leaders communicate a compelling vision for the future. The change process involves moving from Point A to Point B: from the status quo to a desirable, future-goal state.
3. Lead the implementation process—Carefully plan for opportunities to involve the whole team; without their support, full implementation is not possible.
4. Assess results and sustainability of change—The success or failure of change efforts are dependent on how successfully leaders convey a *genuine* feeling that "we are all in this together," and that implementing change is a process that enables all of us to grow and learn together.

CAPACITY BUILDING THROUGH TEACHER LEADERSHIP

Building capacity means different things to different people, especially in an age of increased school accountability. It makes more sense to begin by exploring what capacity building is not. The sustainability of leadership capacity is not anchored in the *followership* of stakeholders, but rather in broad-based *participation* in the work of leadership (Moyo, 2004). Capacity building is not synonymous with shared decision making. Harris and Lambert

(2003) answer the question "How is leadership capacity different from shared decision making?," and just by asking the question, they recognize the importance of the distinction. They define shared decision making as "one aspect of leadership capacity, but learning in schools is about more than decisions. It is about our daily work together—reflection, dialogue, enquiry, and action" (p. 119). They go on to characterize leadership capacity by the way it involves developing new roles and responsibilities. It reframes how teachers interact.

Capacity building is not simple. It is not that it is difficult, but it *is* complex. "If building capacity were simply a matter of imparting knowledge and skills, capacity might be increased by offering workshops" (Floden, Goertz, & O'Day 1995, p. 20). Chaskin (2001) offers four fundamental characteristics of the capacity of a community:

1. A sense of community
2. A level of commitment among community members
3. The ability to solve problems
4. Access to resources

Chaskin notes that to some degree these characteristics may exist in every community, but "there are likely threshold levels of them necessary for a community to accomplish certain ends" (pp. 295–296).

Harris and Lambert (2003) identified five features critical to building leadership capacity in a school; each is "firmly tied to school improvement and pupil achievement" (p. 119). These five critical features are:

1. Broad-based skillful involvement
2. Enquiry-based use of information to inform decisions and practice
3. Roles and responsibilities that reflect broad involvement and collaboration
4. Reflective practice and innovation is the norm
5. High pupil achievement

In an era of intense focus on school improvement and pupil achievement, everyone is searching for the magic bullet to build capacity and squeeze out a few more points on the high stakes assessments. There are sound practices that take a good deal of time and energy to implement, but there are no short cuts which will provide long-term sustainability. The oldest public school in America, Boston Latin School, was founded in 1635; if a magic bullet existed, it most likely would have been discovered in the 377 years since the inception of public education.

ROBERTA EMPOWERS THE FACULTY

It has evolved at Principal Roberta's school that the last faculty meeting of the year is a state-of-the-school address, or what could more accurately be termed a collective "shout-out" of the myriad wins both large and small that can otherwise go unnoticed or underappreciated in the daily operation of a busy school year. This year-end celebration of wins takes about two hours, as it is interrupted by short stories that accompany the praise, and by applause as peers recognize peers.

Wins often take the form of following the initially "hare-brained" idea (explained in chapter 7) from inception to its status as "brilliant," reinforcing the message that every brilliant idea began as a humble "hare-brained" idea. The following are a few typical examples of end-of-the-year shout-outs.

CASE STUDY

Kate—The Reading Teacher

Kate, a reading teacher with a passion for community theatre, approached Principal Roberta with a professional development opportunity she had discovered that promised to show teachers how to use drama as a medium to engage and teach children. This teacher had a vision of one day turning her love of drama into a teaching tool. Following this professional development, the teacher began a drama club at Sorrin School. Five years into this endeavor, the teacher has exceeded her wildest expectation of how her dream would one day manifest itself.

The annual drama club production is now one of the highlights of the school year for many children and their parents, with two separate performances by two separate casts because it is so popular with the budding student actors. A group of teachers support their colleague's dream by helping the new drama director expose students not only to the joys of acting, but also to script writing, set design, costume making, and so on. This highly successful endeavor began as the dream held by one teacher.

Morgan—The First Grade Teacher

Morgan, a first-grade teacher, spoke in casual conversation of a vague notion of inviting a storyteller to address children and parents after school. Roberta offered encouragement and was surprised when the same teacher returned later that day with the school librarian. They were very energized and had fleshed out the idea further into a Family Literacy Night. Within a few days, the art teacher was involved in designing an art component to the evening for the children. The plan was for parents and children to listen to an engaging story together, and then have the children go to another room to work on a related craft; meanwhile, their parents heard about the importance of reading and telling stories and received expert tips from the storyteller.

Family Literacy Night now involves at least a dozen teachers and draws in so many school families that it can no longer be held in the library; in order to accommodate the crowd, it had to be moved to the gymnasium bleachers with mats on the gym floor for the children's seating. Each year, a different literary celebrity is invited to give a presentation, and a cultural grant funds the event. This tradition began when a first-grade teacher who thought it would be nice to bring a storyteller to the school received the encouragement to share her idea.

George—The Paraprofessional

George, a paraprofessional (N.B., in some regions of the country this is referred to as a teacher's aide or teaching assistant) who was a fitness buff, was concerned with the sedentary lifestyle of many of the students with whom he worked. There was one student with special needs with whom this paraprofessional was particularly concerned. The "para" asked if he could come in early and open the gymnasium for a few students to run with this student before homeroom. Within a couple of months, the school had a running club with approximately fifty participants. This culminated in the creation of a widely popular half-mile/mile run on field day for students and staff. The student who originally spurred the para to open the gym in the mornings was one of the last students across the finish line. As the student approached the finish line, faculty and staff lined the racecourse to cheer him on and slap him on the back because it was the first time in his life he had ever run a half mile. If one didn't know better, they would have thought he was about to cross the finish line first at the Olympics. This paraprofessional's idea not only led to teaching about the importance of fitness, but also taught perseverance and acceptance of differences. Everyone who finished the race received a medal, but it was the whole school community cheering the student on that the student will likely remember when he thinks back on that day.

Principal Roberta's school is filled with similar stories about how teacher-leaders have stepped forward to bring their ideas of how to improve the school for students to fruition. It is important to note that this culture is not limited to teachers; school nurses, custodians, and cafeteria workers all have taken leadership roles that contribute to school improvement.

In Summary

Principals are called upon to adopt a new frame from which to view their roles if they hope to create a shift in the paradigm that will positively impact school culture. A cultural change will build the capacity of the school, which in turn will result in an improved experience for all students and, correspondingly, positively impact their achievement.

The old hierarchical top-down model with one leader managing from the top and calling all the shots is no longer viable, except possibly in the smallest of schools. To manage the complexity of the modern schoolhouse, principals will have to adapt their leadership style and distribute leadership tasks with teacher-leaders. This is accomplished by enlisting, not appointing, teacher-leaders to help. Supporting teacher-leaders is about encouraging their full participation, not about demanding their followership. Formally appointing leadership roles does not build a sustainable community of leaders.

The school begins by building sufficient trust for emergent teacher-leaders to identify and share their mental models. These individual mental models are used to build a collective mental model or shared vision. What this looks like will vary from school to school as each school's culture is beginning from a different starting point. Not until there is a clear and concise shared vision will people be committed to change. The power of a community of leaders, teacher-leaders, and principal is in its common beliefs and shared goals.

Chapter Discussion Questions

1. Randy Pausch's first boss saw only brick walls. Think of challenges facing your school and list what you consider to be the brick walls. If you want something badly enough, could you find a solution? Could there be possibilities that you have not yet considered?

2. Sheriff Montoya deputized the town's people to protect a farmer. Who can you, or your principal, deputize, and to do what?

3. Rate on a scale of 1 to 5 (5 representing full implementation) where your school stands in each of McCusker's key challenges for organizational change:
   a. Evaluate the status quo
   b. Articulate a vision
   c. Lead the implementation process
   d. Assess the results and sustainability of change

4. List specific examples from your community for each of the four fundamental characteristics of the capacity of community: a sense of community, a level of commitment among community members, the ability to solve problems, and access to resources.

The Teacher as Leader

Chapter 4   Who Are Teacher-Leaders?
Chapter 5   Where and How Teachers-Leaders Lead
Chapter 6   Learning to Lead

CHAPTER

4

Who Are Teacher-Leaders?

Too often, we shuffle our best teachers into full-time administrative roles, pulling them away from the children who need them most. Too often, we pile "reforms" on teachers without inviting them (and supporting them) to take on meaningful roles in solutions. [It's time we] welcome teacher leaders as partners.

—BERRY, B. (2011a)

This chapter is about *teacher-leaders*: the leaders, if you will, who leaders lead. It describes who teacher-leaders are and who they are not. It looks at their characteristics and examines their motivations. It considers the factors that keep potential teacher-leaders from exercising leadership, and provides suggestions as to how they can overcome those barriers.

Teacher-leaders see themselves, first of all, as teachers. They are educators who want to continue to work as teachers rather than as managers. They also want to invest their know-how and energy beyond the classroom in ways they feel will help improve their school and its instructional effectiveness, their school/community relationships, and the profession at large. This is not to say that over time some may not decide that they can exercise their leadership and affect teaching and learning more directly as an administrator; but until they do, they are teacher-leaders.

Beyond this universal understanding of the term, the concept of teacher-leader manifests itself from school to school and district to district in profound as well as subtle ways: after all, so do the cultures, climates, and policies of the systems in which teachers function as leaders. Consequently, teacher leadership has been variously defined as:

> ". . . the process by which teachers, individually or collectively, influence their colleagues, principals, and other members of the school communities to improve teaching and learning practices with the aim of increased student learning and achievement."
> *(The Center for Comprehensive School Reform and Improvement, 2005, p. 287)*

". . . influencing and engaging colleagues toward improved practice."
(Wasley, 1992, p. 21)

". . . concerned with teachers helping teachers so that teachers can, in turn, better help students. Teacher leadership is helping teachers work together to establish and achieve the goals and objectives of the school."
(Pellicer & Anderson, 1995, p. 22)

".. . . an ethical stance that is based on views of both a better world and the power of teaching to shape meaning systems. It manifests in actions that involve the wider community in the long term. It reaches its potential in contexts where system and school structures are facilitative and supportive."
(Crowther, 1997, p. 15)

". . . a professional commitment and process which influences people to take joint actions toward changes and improved practices that enable achievement of shared educational goals and benefit the common good." *(Forster, 1997, p. 88)*

". . . actions by teachers outside their own classrooms that involve an explicit or implicit responsibility to provide professional development to their colleagues, to influence their communities' or districts' policies, or to act as adjunct district staff to support changes in classroom practices among teachers."
(Miller, Moon, & Elko, 2000, p. 4)

"Whatever the unique job description, *Teacher Leaders* are crucial members of a school or district leadership team, and are personally and professionally responsible for a school's success." *(United States Department of Education, 2012)*

Margolis (2010), chair of the Department of Instruction and Leadership in Education in the School of Education at Duquesne University, refers to teachers leading beyond the classroom in addition to teaching in their classroom as "hybrid" teacher-leaders. Anna, a middle school English language arts (ELA), social studies, and resource teacher in California, also used the term "hybrid." When answering the question "What Are Teachers Most Excited About This Year?," asked by the Center for Teaching Quality's (2011) Teacher Leaders Network to determine what teachers were most looking forward to in the 2011–12 year, Anna replied, "I've been out of my own classroom for the past two years—and in many other classrooms instead as a peer coach, mentor, and co-teacher. This year I'll spend half my time in my classroom and half supporting other teachers on campus. Having a classroom of kids that I get to be with every day is exhilarating (and what I missed most in my former position). I look forward to the challenges of this new hybrid role."

The label "teacherpreneur" has also been equated with teacher-leader. The term is attributed to the Cool Cat Teacher Blog (2006). Vicki Davis, the creator of the Cool Cat Teacher Blog, considers herself a businesswoman as well as a teacher. Here's how she defined teacherpreneurs:

They are the people that movies are made about. They get in trouble with their renegade practices until people realize that they work. Then, they leave teaching and write books, and make movies. We need more of them!

Ariel Sacks, one of a group of educators assembled by the Center for Teaching Quality, referred to teacher leaders as "teacherpreneurs" during a team writing session. Sacks predicted that the schools of 2030 will need growing numbers of teacherpreneurs, which she described as "teacher leaders of proven accomplishment who have a deep knowledge of how to teach, a clear understanding of what strategies must be in play to make schools highly successful, and the skills and commitment to spread their expertise to others—all the while keeping at least one foot firmly in the classroom" (Berry, 2010).

Olsen (2012) titles his blog *Teacher Facilitator Page* because, as he explains, "the activities of a classroom teacher who is a 'teacher leader' . . . are better characterized by the term facilitator than leader." He supports his allegation by citing the Random House Dictionary definition of *facilitate*:

1. to make easier or less difficult; help forward (an action, process, etc.),
2. to assist the progress of (a person)—to make it possible or easier for something to happen.

and the Merriam-Webster Dictionary definition of *facilitator*:

one that facilitates; especially one that helps to bring about an outcome (as learning, productivity, or communication) by providing indirect or unobtrusive assistance, guidance, or supervision.

By permission. From *Merriam-Webster's Collegiate® Dictionary, 11th Edition* © 2013 by Merriam-Webster, Inc. (www.Merriam-Webster.com).

Not so incidentally, Olsen points out that in the "functions" sections of the seven domains of the Model Standards for Teacher Leadership (2011), the verbs foster, promote, facilitate, improve, and advocate are used, but the verb lead is not.

TEACHERS AS LEADERS IN THEIR OWN CLASSROOMS

There once was a man who spent much of his time wandering the world observing its ways. One day, he came across an old woman and asked her if he was on the right path. "You will find out whether you are on the right path when you come to flowing water," said the crone. "Meanwhile," she added, "whenever you learn something new, pick up a pebble as a reminder and put it in your pocket."

One day, the wanderer found himself by a wide river. A tollbooth fronted the bridge that crossed the rapidly flowing water. Gathered around the booth was a group of people. "We are builders," they told him. "We have come to build a city on the other side of the river, but we do not have enough talents to pay the toll needed to cross the bridge."

"I have only these," the wanderer said, and pulled a handful of pebbles from his pocket. When he opened his hand he saw that the pebbles he had collected while learning about the world had turned to talents—more than enough to send the city builders across the river. The wanderer knew then that he had been on the right path all along.

(Based on a story told by Allen [2005] during one of his workshops.)

Often, when we (the authors) think about teachers as leaders in the classroom, Allen's story and how it resonates with Brubaker's definition of leaders comes to mind. Brubaker (2004) defines leaders as those who "use [their] talents to help others identify and use their talents (pp. 71–72)". We especially like Brubaker's definition because it epitomizes what teachers do in the classroom; they use their talents to help students use their own. Yet, if you were to ask a gathering of teachers to raise their hands if they consider themselves leaders, odds are that the response would be minimal.

Those teachers who did not raise their hands have yet to grasp the leadership aspect of their role in the classroom as defined by Brubaker, and by extension, they have yet to grasp their potential as teacher-leaders beyond the classroom.

Yaron (2009), in a study of the perception of the concept of teachers as leaders, suggests that teachers do not see themselves as leaders despite the fact that they seem to attribute leadership qualities to themselves as promulgated in Kouzes and Posner's (2002) criteria of effective leadership.

To dispel the idea that teacher and leader represent two different roles, it would be helpful to consider the Möbius strip as a metaphor. Cut a strip of paper about an inch wide from the long edge of an 8.5″ × 11″ sheet of paper. Print the word TEACHER on one side, like so:

TEACHER

Print LEADER on the other side:

LEADER

We see the two words—"teacher" and "leader"—separated by the thickness of the paper, one word on each side. Our nonhand-raisers tend to think of the roles "teacher" and "leader" as separate, with each on its own side of the education continuum.

Twist the paper strip a half-turn and staple or tape the ends to form a Möbius strip. It will look like this:

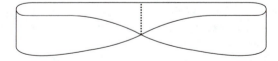

Now the two words are on the same surface of the strip (a Möbius strip has only one surface). When we look at "teacher" and "leader" through the unique lens of the Möbius strip, we see that the two roles are literally on the same side.

With a slight tweak in our perception, we are able to see that teacher and leader are synonymous terms (which is why we hyphenate the two words). They both use their talents to help others use their own.

TEACHERS AS LEADERS BEYOND THE CLASSROOM

When teachers express their leadership beyond the classroom, they serve in one of two fundamental types of roles: formal or informal (Danielson, 2006).

When teachers volunteer or are assigned or recruited to assume leadership in an event or project outside the classroom, they are *formal* teacher-leaders. Typically, formal teacher-leaders manage curriculum projects or facilitate teacher study or professional learning groups. They may also mentor or coach other teachers. Ideally, they receive training geared to their new responsibilities. Formal teacher-leaders play vital roles in most schools—leading, yes, but also supporting collaborative-minded principals.

Informal teacher-leaders, in contrast, emerge spontaneously and organically from the teacher ranks. Instead of being selected, they take the initiative to address a problem or institute a project or program. These teachers have the desire and drive to be proactive. They use their talents to address something they believe in, something that will make a difference: not necessarily in the classroom, but perhaps in the hallways, grounds, or the school community as a whole. As Braden (2011) puts it, "We lead out of our own personal passions and values. Whether or not we are always conscious of them, they are present in our leadership."

Informal teacher-leaders aren't leaders because they have been *assigned* a role or position; rather, they *earn* their leadership through their work with their students, their colleagues, the school, and community. These informal teacher-leaders are teachers first. They emerge from among their teaching colleagues when they see an opportunity for improvement or notice a need. Informal teacher-leaders hold a vision, share it with others, and focus their energy and the energy of others toward the achievement of that vision. Because they are doing something they believe in, and what they are doing sits well with their set of values and is relevant to their lives, they do it better. They do it with passion, and may even change the culture of the school and community in the process. Table 4.1 summarizes formal and informal teacher-leader differences and similarities.

TABLE 4.1 Formal and Informal Teacher-Leaders	
Formal Teacher-Leaders	**Informal Teacher-Leaders**
Volunteer or are assigned or recruited for the role	Emerge spontaneously and organically from the teacher ranks
Typically manage curriculum projects, facilitate teacher study or professional learning groups, or mentor or coach other teachers	Take the initiative to address a problem or institute a project or program within or beyond school borders
Usually take on the role to foster programs or projects with which they agree and/or to support collaborative-minded principals	Have their own vision, share it with others, and focus their energy and the energy of others toward the achievement of that vision
Are drawn to leadership roles because they crave intellectual stimulation, miss opportunities to feel like they were constantly learning, or want to do something that would make a difference in education	
See themselves as teachers who want to continue to work as teachers rather than as administrators; they also want to invest their know-how and energy beyond the classroom in ways they feel will help improve their school and its instructional effectiveness, their school-community relationships, or the profession at large	

WHAT MOTIVATES A TEACHER-LEADER?

Some veteran classroom teachers are drawn to leadership roles because they crave intellectual stimulation, miss opportunities to feel like they are constantly learning, and want to do something that makes a difference in education. Impacting one class of kids each year may not feel like enough. Unless recognized and addressed, such perceptions may result in emotional exhaustion, depersonalization, reduced personal accomplishment, and ultimately burnout and dropout. Anderson and Iwanicki (1984) found that, generally, deficiencies in higher levels of self-actualization needs accounted for a significant amount of burnout among teachers.

Self-actualization is the need to fulfill one's potential (Maslow, 1954). Self-actualization is made up of a variety of qualities, such as the desire to interact with and help—to give as opposed to take; the creative desire to solve problems—particularly those of others (Bishop, 2007); curiosity (Reiss, 2004); and the sense of efficacy—the sense that one has had some impact on others and an effect on the environment (Kollack, 1998). The role of teacher-leader supports an individual's own self-image as an efficacious person (Kollack, 1998).

Fairman and Mackenzie (2012), in a study of seven schools in the state of Maine, found that teachers initiated their own professional learning efforts with the central goal of improving the conditions and outcomes of student learning. Teachers were leading through their strong commitment to continued learning, and by modeling a willingness to take risks, to collaborate, and to question existing practices. Teachers often began with a focus on their own learning and classroom teaching and later moved into other leadership spheres where they collaborated with and influenced colleagues and other stakeholders on a wider scale.

Kelly (2012), a middle school science department chair in Fairfax, Virginia, shares three reasons why she became a teacher-leader.

1. *I wanted more opportunities to have my voice heard.* I'll admit, I have a lot of opinions. Through leadership positions at my school, I am able to voice these opinions to the final decision makers. . . . After becoming a teacher-leader, I found that I was often asked, "What do you think?"
2. *I wanted to impact students outside my classroom.* As a teacher-leader, my impact on student learning has multiplied. By helping and mentoring other teachers in my school or district, my knowledge impacts the students in their classes.
3. *I wanted to grow and learn as a professional.* As a teacher-leader I get opportunities to learn from others and meet new people. I attend district meetings and workshops outside my school where I collaborate and interact with teachers and administrators. I also participate in professional organizations and attend national conferences. Through discussions at these events, I build my own knowledge, which I pass on to teachers in my school.

BARRIERS TO TEACHER LEADERSHIP

Historically, lack of a culture and traditions that would serve to empower teachers has created an expectation that the only job of teachers is to teach students, and the classroom is the legitimate extent of a teacher's involvement and responsibility (Sacken, 1994). For a teacher working in such an environment—whether real or perceived—who is considering the risk of taking on the role of teacher-leader, it places him or herself on the perplexing horns of a dilemma. After all, risk taking can be foolish—even harmful. Yet taking a chance is sometimes called for in order to pursue a vision or address a need. Acting on the desire to extend leadership beyond the classroom can be risky. A lack of support and encouragement from school administrators and teaching colleagues often poses the biggest obstacle to informal teacher-leaders. A hostile culture can breed resentment and even antagonism from colleagues toward teachers attempting to exhibit leadership. Teachers aspiring to emerge as leaders may feel that they may not be accepted and respected, and may even blame the administration for failing to support their leadership aspirations, thereby engendering an even more hostile environment. On another level, deciding to take on a leadership role may carry with it a feeling of discomfort because doing so violates a perceived notion of the egalitarian relationship among teachers. Even in the arena of formal teacher leadership, the selection of lead teachers by the administration may violate the "equal status" tradition of teachers and breed resentment and hostility.

Aspiring teacher-leaders might well ask themselves, "Do I dare take the risk?" The answer is a resounding "Yes!," provided their decision to do so is an informed one. Portner (2002, pp. 46–47) cautions that before teachers decide to risk, they would do well to take the time to inform their decision by testing it against the following two criteria:

1. ***Look at the moral and ethical implications of taking the risk.*** In the medical profession, doctors take the Hippocratic oath, during which they agree to do no harm. The same holds true for teacher-leaders. While we all may make mistakes, our laudable efforts to lead do not include the right to threaten our own or someone else's physical, emotional, or psychological health or safety, or to infringe on the rights of others. If taking a particular risk may cause harm, don't take the risk.

2. ***Consider whether taking that risk would violate the formal or informal policies, practices, and perceptions in your school.*** Most schools operate within a set of official or formal policies and procedures that fall under such categories as curriculum standards, discipline protocols, and ordering supplies. There are also unofficial practices working within virtually all schools that have as much to do with how a school functions as do the formal ones. These are *culture* (this is the way we do things around here) and *tradition* (this is the way we've always done them). So if taking the risk flies in the face of such issues, don't do it without first considering the consequences. Always let wisdom and decorum prevail.

Costa and Kallick (2000) suggest that the teacher-leader manage his or her impulse to take a risk by asking:

- Is this a good time to take a risk and pose a challenge?
- What is the intensity of this need? Does it need to be handled now or can it wait?
- Am I in the right frame of mind to say something, or will I become too emotional?
- If I speak up, who or what else will this affect? What is the ripple effect?
- If I bring this issue up, do I have an action plan thought out? Can I support an individual through the changes I would like to see made? Do I have a game plan in mind?
- Can I say what I want to say and still project acceptance of the person?
- If I do bring up the concern, is there enough time to really deal with it, or will it just cause problems?

They go on to caution the teacher-leader to manage his or her passivity by asking:

- How important is it for the students or other staff that I bring this up?
- Is what is going on in the classroom physically unsafe, academically unsound, or emotionally damaging to students or colleagues?
- What might happen if I didn't have the conversation?
- What am I trying to accomplish, and if I speak up, will it move me toward or away from that goal?
- No matter the outcome, is this something I have to say because I have to say it?
- By my silence, does this person think I agree with his or her perspective or behavior? Is that OK?

One of the most important skills one can cultivate as a leader is the ability to separate action from reaction. Thinking before you speak and then speaking up when you feel it is truly important are the first steps to becoming an effective leader.

Anthony (2006), a Library Media Specialist at Marblehead Veterans Middle School in Marblehead, Massachusetts, relates how she took a risk and challenged the status quo. When Ms. Anthony started her job in Marblehead, she found that the library and media center had been newly expanded and renovated, but students had too little time and freedom to use its wealth of resources. Near the end of the school year, she approached Principal Richard Davidson and told him that with all we know about creating print-rich environments and how much practice students need to be successful readers, it is imperative that a school library give students as much barrier-free access as possible. She asked the principal straight out, "Did you build this very expensive facility so that kids could visit just once a week?"

Davidson agreed that students come first. He accepted the idea of open access replacing scheduled library classes. At an end-of-year staff meeting, teachers agreed to try open access for one year and then assess its effectiveness. The next fall, library use had been transformed. The library was open to all students at all times while school was in session. Library use dramatically increased and the flexible scheduling encouraged teachers to collaborate on projects.

One deterrent to undertaking the role of teacher-leader is the "impostor phenomenon," a self-imposed feeling of inadequacy and a fear that others may discover how little one really knows (Clance, 1985). The syndrome is a natural process that can be experienced by both prospective and veteran teacher-leaders. Even when initial feelings of confusion and inadequacy are dispelled, they may reoccur as the teacher-leader encounters unexpected problems. Ironically, the teacher-leader's reluctance to cast herself as an expert can undermine others' perceptions of her ability to serve as a resource. If teachers view the teacher-leader as lacking expert knowledge, there is little incentive to seek the teacher-leader's advice or guidance (Mangin, 2005).

Linton (2011) describes how becoming a teacher-leader challenged his collegial relationships.

> *One day, I was a regular teacher with a regular teaching load going through the routines of a regular school year. The next, I was a leader and professional developer, working to institute change in the sometimes difficult to grasp field of 21st century learning. I went from teaching alongside my colleagues to "change agent"; garnering a wide range of emotional responses from them. Some colleagues politely excused themselves from the process—the equivalent of, "that's*

nice dear, good luck with that." Some were openly hostile to the process. Some reacted with excitement before realizing that by taking part in the project they had moved outside their comfort zone. Some went along for the ride without ever buying in. A few were stalwart supporters every step of the way.

Everyone involved went through their own emotional journey of doubts and frustrations, victories and challenges. When I agreed to the position of teacher leader, I had little understanding of the emotional side of the change process or that by taking on the leadership role (formal or not) I had placed myself in the eye of the storm. Navigating the emotional impact of the change process was, without question, one of the greatest challenges of teacher leadership.

DO UNIONS PRESENT A BARRIER TO TEACHER LEADERSHIP?

A frequently cited barrier to grassroots teacher leadership is the supposedly pervasive, even controlling, role of the National Education Association and the American Federation of Teachers in the work lives of the nation's teachers. Barth (2007) echoes this perspective by pointing out that "[s]ome unions don't look kindly at teachers who take on additional leadership functions without pay. They set and enforce limits on teachers' allocation of uncompensated time and draw attention to those who breach the limits" (p. 16).

The Report of the Task Force on Teacher Leadership (2001, p. 12) explains that "[t]he fact is that most of the tangible gains teachers achieved in the second half of the 20th century *would not have materialized without union activism and leadership.*" The long-run effect of the unions' presence has been to elevate the professional stature and self-regard of teachers and to strengthen the potential for teachers to lead. As teacher-leaders gain more responsibilities and influence over their schools and profession, school boards and teacher bargaining units are beginning to consider how teacher-leadership should be recognized and compensated.

Here are two examples of union support of teacher-leaders. First, the United Educators of San Francisco, after conducting a successful year-long pilot project in 2011–2012, expanded its Teacher Leaders Program by offering a $1,000 stipend to encourage more teachers to step out of the classroom on occasion and help shape education policy that affects the profession both in San Francisco and nationally.

Second, the Los Angeles Unified School District's Teacher Effectiveness Task Force—which included the district's bargaining partners as well as parents, community representatives, private sector leaders, higher education partners, teachers, and administrators—created positions and/or roles that provide significant promotional opportunities for effective teachers to remain in the classroom part of the time, while bringing their expertise to other teachers at their schools and/or throughout the District. Possible roles include teacher-leaders to facilitate the individual growth planning process and teachers-leaders who perform observations of teacher practice. With additional responsibilities and time commitments, such roles would come with enhanced compensation.

OVERCOMING BARRIERS

Teacher-leaders who create and shape their own roles may actually receive more support and experience greater success than those who are less willing and able to take the initiative. In practical terms, this means proactively developing the support of teachers and administrators. How does one go about gaining support? Portner (2001) suggests that one way is through application of this quasi-equation: ***Beliefs + Expectations + Reward (leads to) Support***.

Beliefs is agreement with the efficacy and value of the teacher-leader's actions and goals. When we support something we believe in—when what we support sits well within our set of values and is relevant to our lives—we support it with passion. This is why resonance with beliefs is part of the support equation. If teacher-leaders want the support of colleagues, they need to help others see how doing so can also support their own beliefs and values, both as individuals and as educators.

Expectations is confidence that the teacher-leader's efforts will result in positive outcomes. Most people will need to have tangible reasons to feel confident that a teacher-leader's efforts will succeed before they will grant their support. One way to engender confidence in eventual success is to provide the opportunity for potentially supportive people to participate in some aspects of the teacher-leader's plans or activities. Another way to raise people's expectations for success is to share with them some of the research and anecdotal material about the project.

Reward is the perception that support of the teacher-leader's efforts will result in one's own personal, professional, or philosophical growth. When an administrator or teacher considers investing time and energy in supporting a teacher-leader, somewhere in their decision-making process—consciously or not—they will ask themselves, "What will I or my organization get out of this?" The rewards are not necessarily self-serving ones. Our behaviors and decisions are often determined by our desire to satisfy less tangible needs. Supporting a teacher-leader may address a need in a variety of ways. Maslow (1954) postulates seven levels in his hierarchy of needs that affect human behavior, five of which are relevant to the support equation:

- Social needs (affiliation, belonging, feeling part of something)
- Esteem needs (recognition, respect, feeling of worth)
- Need for self-actualization (putting abilities to work, using talents)
- Need to know and understand (intellectual curiosity, thirst for knowledge)
- Esthetic needs (order and balance, satisfying relationships)

All three factors on the left side of the equation, Beliefs, Expectations, and Rewards, must be in operation in order for genuine Support to occur; although, of course, some may grant their support simply because they like and respect the teacher-leader.

Teacher-leaders can prevent or overcome barriers to their leadership efforts by empowering their principal to be a leader of leaders. They can let the principal know their vision, show how their actions will resonate with the principal's beliefs and values, indicate how and where they have or can get the wherewithal to accomplish their leadership vision, detail how their actions as a teacher-leader will benefit students and the school, and ask for and thank them for their support.

TEACHER-LEADERSHIP BEHAVIORS

What kinds of behaviors characterize a teacher-leader? Teacher-leaders take certain actions. They hold a vision, communicate it to others, and act to achieve the vision. They place a value on providing assistance. They model collegiality as a mode of work, make provisions for their own continuous learning, and encourage others to provide leadership to their peers.

In an ad seeking a teacher to lead its gifted student support programs, the Oakleigh-Mulgrave and Mill Park-Greensborough areas of Melbourne, Australia listed the following among the behavioral criteria preferred for the position:

- Good communicator
- Well-organized
- Professional leadership skills
- Ability to provide ongoing growth and support for your people

These and other teacher-leadership abilities do not happen by chance. They happen when teachers commit to their leadership vision and plan for (rather than hope for) success. Teachers may find that success depends upon learning and applying a variety of leadership skills, such as:

- Building trust and developing rapport
- Diagnosing organizational conditions
- Dealing with processes
- Managing the work
- Building skills and confidence in others
- Uncovering teacher leadership

Ackerman and Mackenzie (2006) see teacher-leaders as "[having to] contend with several challenges dictated by the status quo, such as the antiquated notions of leadership, teacher isolation, and the conservatism that so often reigns in schools. Succeeding as a teacher leader means staying true to one's beliefs, coupling confidence with humility, and being willing to work with colleagues to improve student learning" (p. 66).

The role of teacher-leader need not be a permanent one. A teacher may decide to exercise leadership one year but not another. Even if a teacher continues as a leader, the focus of teacher leadership can vary over time. Once a teacher has demonstrated leadership skills and established credibility with colleagues, she is recognized as a teacher-leader regardless of where she applies those abilities.

In Summary

There are nearly endless definitions of teacher-leader. What remains central is the repudiation of the dichotomous mind-set: *You are a teacher or a principal, a leader or a follower.* The removal of this "either-or" barrier to teacher leadership brings a far greater array of skills and strengths than would have otherwise been available to bear on student achievement, school effectiveness, and professional growth.

Every competent teacher is a leader in her or his own classroom by virtue of the fact that they do what leaders do; they use their talents and abilities to help others—in this case, their students—to use their own. It is when a teacher exercises leadership beyond the classroom yet remains a teacher that he or she becomes a teacher-leader.

Teachers are motivated to lead beyond the classroom because they may feel they have something to offer their colleagues, school, community, or profession. Some teachers on the verge of burnout but wanting to remain in the profession look to leadership opportunities as a path to higher levels of intellectual or professional stimulation.

Emergent teacher-leaders sometimes face barriers to teacher leadership. They may find that they receive little or no support from administrators, and may even be discouraged by them. Some teachers considering undertaking teacher-leadership opportunities may feel, rightly or wrongly, that they are not "good enough" or that they will be looked down upon by their peers for aspiring to a role that is contrary to a culture of egalitarian peer relationships.

Emergent teacher-leaders can overcome these and other barriers by empowering peers and administrators. They can avoid being self-blocked in their aspirations by showing how their actions resonate with others' beliefs, will meet their expectations, and reward their involvement and support.

Although many teacher-leaders may have and be able to apply some leadership skills, most of those skills and behaviors need to be developed. Developing and/or enhancing such skills are vital to effective teacher-leadership. Chapter 6 examines the professional development of teacher-leaders.

Chapter Discussion Questions

1. Teacher leadership in practice is an ambiguous concept with shifting boundaries and unclear rules.
   a. What is your personal concept of teacher leadership?
      • Make a list of ideas that indicate what teacher leadership is. For example, teacher leadership is collaboration.
      • Consider and write a list of what teacher leadership is not. For example, teacher leadership is not a decision-making process, or teacher leadership is not a matter of simply delegating tasks.
   b. After the process of identifying personal assumptions is complete, develop a shared understanding of teacher leadership.
   c. How are our assumptions similar?
   d. How are our assumptions different?

(Adapted from "What Is Teacher Leadership?," an article by Evelyn Cortez-Ford published 08/11/2006 in Education World®. Retrieved 11/15/2012 from http://www.educationworld.com/a_admin/columnists/cortez-ford/cortez-ford001.shtml)

2. How might Brubaker's definition of leaders, ". . . those who use [their] talents to help others identify and use their talents" (Brubaker, 2004, pp. 71–72) apply to a teacher being a *leader of leaders in the classroom*?

3. Suppose you were a teacher-leader who wants to form a parent advisory committee to provide recommendations regarding extra-curriculum activities for students. What might you say or what resources might you provide to a principal regarding:
   a. Beliefs
   b. Expectations
   c. Rewards
   in order to gain her or his support?

5 Where and How Teacher-Leaders Lead

If your actions inspire others to dream more, learn more, do more and become more, you are a leader.

—JOHN QUINCY ADAMS

This chapter is about how and where teachers reach out beyond the four walls of a classroom and *inspire others to dream more, learn more, do more, and become more.* Teacher leadership is no longer an alien concept in education. It is generally expected that schools provide leadership opportunities for teachers and that teachers engage in leadership activities of their own volition. Here are a few abbreviated examples of where and how teachers lead.

Arlene J. is a first-year middle school teacher in a semiurban Midwest district. At the beginning of the school year and for the first month, she felt confined to her classroom and sure she was shortchanging her students. Then she decided to take the initiative and do more for her students. She formed a Drama Club and put on a musical for the school year. She also decided to institute an after school tutoring program.

Special education instructor Christine K. and kindergarten teacher Kevin B. were chosen by a panel of parents and school staff as teacher-leaders to replace the principal at an elementary school in Portland, Maine. They work part-time as teachers and part-time as administrators. The school was the first in the country to transition from a traditional, administratively led school into a teacher-led school, where committees of teachers make decisions and two teacher-leaders run the day-to-day operations of the school.

Michael F., a Massachusetts elementary school teacher, sits on his local school board, speaking for children in the district where he lives. Holly B., a National Board Certified Teacher from Louisiana, sits on her state's Board of Elementary and Secondary Education.

The preceding examples of teacher leadership are indicative of the variety of roles assumed by teacher-leaders. The diversity of teacher leadership activities is extensive, and instances of where and how teachers can lead are as varied as teachers themselves (Lieberman, 1992; Loucks-Horsley, Hewson, Love, & Stiles, 1998).

When teachers volunteer or are assigned or recruited to assume leadership outside the classroom, they are *formal* teacher-leaders. *Informal* teacher-leaders, in contrast, emerge spontaneously and organically from the teacher ranks. Instead of being selected, they take the initiative to address a problem or institute a project or program.

Teacher-leaders, both formal and informal, exercise their leadership within several areas. Lord and Miller (2000, p. 3) have categorized teacher-leaders as working with

- Individual teachers in classroom settings
- Groups of teachers in workshops or comparable professional development settings
- Teachers, administrators, community members, or students on issues or programs that indirectly support classroom teaching and learning experiences
- Various constituents on the task du jour

We have condensed these four categories into two broader ones:

1. School practices and policies
2. District or community issues and concerns

And added a third:

3. Educational or professional issues beyond school, district, or community

Each of these three areas represents a large array of activities, and there are teacher-leaders who are engaged in more than one activity within a given area and/or in activities in multiple areas.

TEACHERS EXERCISE LEADERSHIP AROUND ISSUES OF SCHOOL PRACTICES AND POLICIES

Leadership within one's own school can develop in several ways and take many forms. Typically, principals make decisions about how teacher-leaders spend their time and what responsibilities they assume. In some schools, teacher-leaders are asked or informally take it upon themselves to use their own professional judgment in determining what they do and how they do it. For example, when a teacher is challenged by an aspect of the Common Core, he or she may turn first to a peer looked upon as a teacher-leader and then later to their school administrator for guidance.

Here is how Robyn J., an advanced placement (AP) language and composition teacher at a diverse high school in the suburbs of Washington, DC, took the initiative to become a teacher-leader in her school. Robyn's class of approximately 35 students did not reflect the diversity of the school's population. School policy stipulated that in order to take an AP class in eleventh grade, students had to take an honors class in tenth grade, and Robyn saw that as a problem. She decided to challenge that policy and let any interested student take her class. She told her principal that she wanted to try this new approach, and showed him research suggesting that the number of AP classes a student takes in high school is a more accurate predictor of college success than a student's grade point average. She also detailed her plans to support the students. The principal had been considering making such a policy change in the school himself, but many staff members were resistant. He decided to support Robyn and charged her with the task of showing the rest of the staff that this approach could work. She agreed, carried out her plan, shared its process and data with colleagues along the way, and within a year, earned their support and cooperation.

Roger W., a veteran sixth-grade teacher in Amherst, Massachusetts, acted on the result of an informal conversation with another teacher and instituted a successful collaborative initiative that resulted in a district-wide Social Justice Commitment Position Statement that has become a guiding principle for the district's curriculum.

Danielson (2007) tells of Maria, a high school Spanish teacher, who noticed that there weren't good opportunities for her to meet with and learn from other Spanish teachers in the area. The state organization of language teachers had not recruited many members in her school or in neighboring schools. Maria decided to begin a chapter of the American Association of Teachers of Spanish and Portuguese in her area. She sent email notices to teachers in other schools and scheduled an organizational meeting. Although response was slow at first, over the course of several years the chapter became vibrant. Before long, members were scheduling visits to one another's schools and preparing presentations for the state conference.

In Mesa, Arizona's Carson Junior High School, teacher-leader Sabine W. not only teaches math and reading to students, she also teaches other staff members how to be better teachers. Designated a "master teacher," Sabine teaches an instructional or learning strategy during an hour-long meeting once a week to small groups of teachers throughout the day. She then follows up by observing teachers and providing them with feedback. In addition to coaching teachers, she provides demonstration lessons and field-tests new learning strategies.

The Math and Science Leadership Academy (MSLA) of Denver, Colorado is a public, teacher-led school working to meet the needs of a diverse population through redefining traditional teacher and administrator roles. MSLA, which first opened in 2009, serves approximately 250 students in kindergarten through third grade with a staff of teachers who, in addition to teaching for at least a portion of their day, also fulfill the administrative duties typically performed by principals, curriculum specialists, and mentors.

For the most part, the activities of teacher-leaders within their schools can be grouped into two categories:

- Working with individual teachers, usually in classroom settings
- Working with teachers, administrators, community members, and/or students on issues or programs that indirectly support classroom experiences

TEACHER-LEADERS WORK WITH INDIVIDUAL COLLEAGUES

Typically, schools tend to rely heavily on administrators or supervisors to support sound instructional practice through classroom observations and feedback. However, they are limited in their perspective when it comes to familiarity with the day-to-day intricacies of classroom life. Administrative and supervisory voices need to be coupled with the voices of peers who can provide the specialized perspective of a master teacher firmly planted in classroom practice. This calls for hybrid roles in which teacher-leaders spend a portion of their time working with students in their own classrooms, and spend another part of their time on efforts to improve teaching and learning in the classrooms of their peers.

Within such a role, a teacher-leader might go into a colleague's classroom and teach his or her students once or twice in order to demonstrate a specific type of instruction. Blase and Blase (2006) found that such interaction with peers enhanced teachers' self-efficacy (teachers' belief in their own abilities and their capacity to successfully solve teaching and learning problems) as they reflected on practice and grew together. They also found that such collaboration encouraged "a bias for action" on the part of teachers (p. 22).

Harrison and Killion (2007) identified 10 roles for locally involved teacher-leaders that are generally carried out in the classroom. These include: "Mentors serve as role models; acclimate new teachers to a new school; and advise new teachers about instruction, curriculum, procedure, practices, and politics" (p. 74). Mentoring can take many forms that may include modeling instruction, observing a teacher teaching a class and offering feedback, and serving as an instructional coach. The mentor is not only concerned with instructional and organizational needs, but also lends emotional and moral support to alleviate the stresses inherent in being a new teacher.

The National Education Association–New Mexico and American Federation of Teachers' joint legislative goals of 2011, for example, support the establishment of programs under which all beginning teachers in the state would be assigned a mentor. The pertinent goal reads as follows: "The legislature must fund district induction and mentoring programs for teachers, including mentorship programs for all new teachers and voluntary peer intervention programs. These programs must be delivered by trained mentors compensated for their work" (p. 3).

Serving as a peer coach is another avenue for teacher leadership. A peer coach is similar to a mentor, except that each teacher in the pair—who are not necessarily novices—functions as mentor and as protégé to each other at different times. As in mentoring, classroom visits are not evaluative or prescriptive, they are diagnostic and constructive, allowing teachers to experiment and take risks without fear of judgment. Peer coaches take turns observing each other and discussing observed instructional behaviors, actions, and practices, which can include giving feedback on plans, lessons, instruction, classroom presence, and classroom management.

Teacher-leaders also help their colleagues by sharing instructional resources such as Web sites, instructional materials, articles, books, lesson plans, and assessment tools; and by helping colleagues implement effective teaching strategies such as differentiating instruction or planning lessons in partnership with fellow teachers (Marzano, Pickering, & Pollock, 2001), exploring which instructional methodologies are appropriate for the school, and sharing findings with colleagues. As is true with the roles of mentor and coach, the instructional specialist's role is also nonsupervisory.

A Sequenced Program of Classroom Support

In a district studied by Lord and Miller (2000), a teacher-leader worked with a teacher who was just starting to implement a new mathematics curriculum. The teacher-leader began by demonstrating a lesson. She taught the lesson in the teacher's classroom while the teacher observed. The demonstration was followed by discussion with the teacher about the lesson's goals, its components, and the challenges it posed for students or the teacher. Next, the teacher-leader observed while the teacher taught a lesson, again followed by a debriefing and critique session in which the teacher-leader offered feedback and elicited reactions from the teacher. Beyond this sequence of demonstrate-debrief-observe-debrief, the teacher-leader tailored the next steps to the needs of this classroom teacher—in this case, team teaching a new type of lesson, continuing to observe and debrief, and assisting in lesson planning.

TEACHER-LEADERS WORK WITH SCHOOL-BASED GROUPS

Danielson (2007) shares the experience of Jennifer, a high school history teacher, who was troubled by her students' responses to tests and papers. Jennifer read their work and provided thoughtful feedback. But when she returned their papers, the students seemed interested only in the grade, and some students would decline to turn in work altogether if they knew it was going to be late, believing that it was not "worth it" to complete it.

Jennifer invited interested teachers from across the school to join her in exploring alternate approaches to grading. They met for an entire school year, and each teacher conducted systematic discussions with their students. Toward the end of the year, the group made a recommendation to the entire faculty; as a result, the school piloted a different grading system the following year that incorporated formative assessment and student self-assessment. At the end of 3 years, the school's approach to grading was considerably different; the teachers were convinced that the new system resulted in greater student buy-in and commitment to high-quality work.

A few years ago, a Dumas, Arkansas high school principal demonstrated the concept of putting decisions involving students in the hands of those who are most capable of making those decisions: teachers. He was considering the possibility of initiating a block schedule. He identified and appointed a committee of teacher-leaders to investigate the idea, visit other schools, collect research information, and present its findings to the entire faculty. The faculty then debated the issue and eventually voted to change to block scheduling.

Boyd-Dimock and McGree (1995) describe another initiative undertaken by Dumas High School: the Ventures in Education (VIE) program. VIE was designed to encourage students to take 4 years each of mathematics, science, English, and social studies, 2 years of a foreign language, and other challenging elective courses. Gerri Appleberry, a Dumas High School teacher, was chosen by the VIE committee as its chair. The high levels of poverty in the district and the students' limited opportunities to attend universities initially spurred Appleberry's interest in the VIE program. Her vision was that students would increase their academic performance and self-confidence.

Appleberry has been a driving force of implementation. As one of her colleagues noted, ". . . she's in charge because she was willing to be in charge. If she had not been in charge, this program might not have gone . . . I mean you're talking about time to teach school and still work on this." Another colleague remarked, ". . . we're behind her, we're there, but you've got to have that leader."

From the beginning, Appleberry believed community support was essential to the successful implementation of the program. She initially built support by contacting parents individually. She also enlisted and received the support of the Chamber of Commerce and the Lions Club. Over time, this support paid off.

Barth (2001) notes that there are at least ten areas, all of which have an impact on teacher and student relationships, where teacher involvement is actually essential to the health of a school:

- Choosing textbooks and instructional materials
- Shaping the curriculum
- Setting standards for student behavior
- Deciding whether students are tracked into special classes
- Designing staff development and in-service programs
- Setting promotion and retention policies
- Deciding on school budgets
- Evaluating teacher performance
- Selecting new teachers
- Selecting new administrators

In Boston, Massachusetts, the Carlton Viveiros Elementary School and Henry Lord Middle School have joined three other Boston schools in a partnership with Teach Plus, a Boston-based organization, to recruit, select, and support experienced teachers for low-performing schools. Teachers who participate in the program continue to serve as full-time classroom educators while also taking on formal and informal leadership roles within their schools. Teacher-leaders lead teams of teachers, facilitate team meetings, and lead the work of using data to help instruct their teams.

Many of these and similar activities are carried out in school-based groups which are as diverse as the teachers who participate in them. These groups or teams can be informal and low-key, like a coffee klatch, designed to relieve the daily stress of teaching. Or they can be highly structured inquiry groups with detailed expectations for participants, and facilitated by one or more teacher-leaders. Such groups function around collaborative discussions informed by the expertise of knowledgeable, caring staff members who understand the dynamics of the school community and student needs. The Professional Learning Community is an example of such a structured group.

Professional Learning Communities

DuFour (2006) defines a professional learning community (PLC) as "a group of people working interdependently toward the same goal," and coming to decisions that all can support. Although an essential element of a PLC is its interdependence, it nevertheless relies on and cultivates teacher leadership and facilitation (Grossman, Wineburg, & Woolworth, 2000). The PLC leader/facilitator's role is to help participants collaborate effectively, work as a team, and take collective responsibility for the group's outcomes.

The Fairmont, West Virginia public schools list the following among qualifications and responsibilities in its PLC Leader Description, Recruitment, and Application (2012):

- Ability to focus and keep a team focused on the PLC goals and process
- Consensus building skills

- Chair teacher (PLC) teams
- Call meetings
- Set agenda
- Monitor participation
- Facilitate collaborative decision making
- Create management process for supply, capital, and event planning

Ferriter (2012) cautions, however, ". . . that there is no simple formula to determining who is going to make a good teacher leader in a learning community. That's because different teams will need different kinds of leadership at different times—so a teacher who exerts significant influence and points a team in the right direction early in their work together may not have the right set of skills to move the same team forward after it has worked together successfully for a while." Ferriter goes on to offer the following ways to identify potential leaders and to create the right conditions for teachers leading learning teams to be successful. These include:

- Look for connected teachers who have a strong commitment to your school's central principles.
- Identify the different types of skills that individual teachers bring to the leadership table.
- Make sure that there are discovery- *and* delivery-oriented teachers on each learning team.

Although there's not a single set of criteria for determining who the teacher-leaders in your learning community will be, the good news is that there are a lot of opportunities for different teachers to lead at different times.

Other types of school-based groups operate using the interdependent focus of a professional learning community. Such teams include:

INTERDISCIPLINARY TEAMS   Interdisciplinary teams are a type of team teaching in which two or more teachers within a grade level who specialize in different subjects share the same students—usually for extended blocks of core instructional time—and plan and teach together to integrate their branches of knowledge. Although there is generally no designated leader, team members informally assume the role under various situations, such as at times when their expertise is sought.

Ideally, students assigned to interdisciplinary teams gain insight into the logical relationships between the various curricular areas and receive classroom assignments that combine the knowledge and skills derived from their teachers' specific areas of expertise. These teams often share the same schedule and the same area of the building. For teachers, teams provide a collaborative and supportive work group. For students, teams offer stable relationships with teachers and peers.

Juvonen (2004) describes three advantages of interdisciplinary teaching for students. First, because teachers share the same groups of students they can discuss the strengths and weaknesses of individual students, making it easier to meet their needs. Second, interdisciplinary teams of teachers can facilitate connections across different disciplines. Finally, there are more opportunities for positive peer and teacher-student relationships because teachers on the same team teach the same groups of students.

DEPARTMENTAL TEAMS Departmental teams include teachers who teach the same content (for example, science), but may not teach the same grade level. Departmental teams help to ensure consistency in delivering grade-level, standards-based content. The Team Leader maintains a calendar of team activities and the team database (on testing results and other team data), and represents the team to administration. Team members can establish other responsibilities to organize themselves according to major goals. For example, it is imperative to keep a record of every meeting because we tend to have selective memories, especially when we are passionate about an issue. An accurate record of what was discussed and what was decided can be helpful in case of future disagreement, as well as in bringing people who missed the meeting up to speed. A Team Recorder takes minutes of each meeting, and sends a summary of the minutes to other content teachers, librarians, and resource teachers.

TEAM LEADERSHIP ISSUES A team can rotate leadership or select a permanent leader from among its members. Team leadership can also be assumed by the strongest or most vocal person on the team. Sometimes, the "egalitarian" culture of a school's faculty can prevent teachers from accepting another teacher's authority. "Let's share leadership" may be a way for individual teachers to avoid stepping into leadership roles. Should a teacher-leader step forward, the unverbalized yet potentially disruptive response may be, "Who are you to tell me what to do?"

Troen and Boles (2011b) identify leadership as one of five conditions exhibited by good teams (the others are task focus, collaborative climate, personal accountability, and structures and processes). They posit that a good team encourages leadership for all its members rather than having the leadership role be undertaken reluctantly, forced upon a member, or assumed by the strongest or most vocal person on the team, and that teams function best when leadership roles are available to all team members at one time or another.

Newmann and Associates (1996) found that school teams with strong leaders paid attention to key facets of both school culture and structure. They set the tone by modeling active learning, investing time in the process, and showing respect for the ideas of others (Zepeda, 1999).

Lambert (2003) developed a rubric of emerging teacher leadership that provides a way to measure a teacher-leader's progress. The rubric describes the characteristics of leadership behavior at the levels of the teacher's adult development application, communication or dialog abilities, collaboration skills, and proficiency in organization development.

THE PRINCIPAL'S ROLE IN SCHOOL TEAMS

Should a principal be a member of a school team? In most cases, the answer is "no." However, when a principal forms or encourages the formation of a teacher team, she has a responsibility to assure that the group has the time, support, and capacity to do what she is asking it to do. Hord and Hirsh (2009, pp. 22–23) list several ways that principals can support teams.

> ***Emphasize to teachers that you know they can succeed—together.*** Let teachers know you believe they have the expertise to work together and that you expect and look forward to them pooling that expertise to achieve the group's goal.

Expect teachers to keep knowledge fresh. Let teachers know you expect them to work together to keep their skills up-to-date in order to increase their effectiveness as a team.

Guide communities toward self-governance. Although you may arrange things at first, urge team members early on to assume prominent roles, share decision-making, and encourage other members to take the lead.

Make data accessible. One element of an effective team is its ability to use data for decision making. Where applicable, make data on the team's task available. You may need to help staff members acquire skills needed to interpret data.

Teach discussion and decision-making skills. Help teachers develop skills to talk and make decisions together—they should learn the difference between *dialogue* and *discussion*. Dialogue—in which members share their knowledge, feelings, or biases—is preferable when the goal of the conversation is to help participants understand one another. Discussion is a good choice when the goal is to make a decision about a course of action.

Show teachers the research. Research indicates that teachers reap benefits from exercising collective responsibility for such things as student success, increased understanding of teachers' roles in helping students achieve, and professional renewal.

Take time to build trust. Team activities are more effective when mutual trust exists between the team members and the principal, as well as among the teachers themselves. Providing teachers with assistance in conducting appropriate conversations, making decisions, and managing conflict will help strengthen trust.

Adapted from "The Principal's Role in Supporting Learning Communities" by S.M. Hord and S.A. Hirsch, in the February 2009 issue of Educational Leadership, 66(5), pp. 22–23. Used with permission. Learn more about ASCD at www.ascd.org.

Supporting teams in these ways can be a challenge for a school administrator. Assisting teams and keeping track of their progress requires a significant investment of time and effort. Elmore (2000) suggests that most administrators respond to this challenge with one of the following three approaches:

1. They devote all of their assistance to the most problematic groups—those that have less capable teacher-leaders, weak content knowledge, or dysfunctional group dynamics.
2. They attempt to attend and manage every meeting.
3. They simply back off and serve as a buffer to protect teachers from distractions and trust team leaders to facilitate productive work.

A principal can be an essential member of a team when the team includes parents and community members as well as teachers, counselors, social workers, and aides, or school food, transportation, or maintenance staff. The principal's membership and support of such partnership groups gives its members the administrative endorsement needed for them to devote adequate time and attention to its tasks. Most of the time, the principal does not chair such a team, but does provide important information about the school, curriculum, and funding that contribute to team deliberations (Hord & Hirsh, 2009).

Recognizing that teams are only as effective as their team culture, a principal might include team members in interviews for prospective new hires. Sometimes, considering whether a qualified candidate will "fit" the team personality can help to avoid dysfunction later.

TEACHERS LEAD IN AREAS OF DISTRICT OR COMMUNITY ISSUES AND CONCERNS

Teacher-leaders have a voice in shaping their district or community concerns, programs, and policies when they participate in such activities as the one instituted by the superintendent of the Poudre School District in Fort Collins, Colorado. The superintendent asked a group of teacher-leaders from around the district to meet twice a year as a council to offer advice to administration on key issues, including district initiatives and cultivation of teacher leadership. During one meeting, for example, the council reviewed the book *Leading for Instructional Improvement* authored by Fink and Markholt (2011), which outlines five dimensions for teaching and learning. Through facilitated discussion, teachers considered how the framework could be useful to them as instructors, in their grade level or department professional learning opportunities, at their schools, and across the district. Additionally, teachers provided guidance on how the framework could be used as a tool for evaluation and still retain its usefulness for professional development.

Teachers can also lead in their surrounding community by teaching adult education courses in their areas of specialty, by participating in community functions to show their support, or by attending community meetings to keep abreast of concerns. Speaking at school board meetings, attending PTA meetings, or serving as liaisons between the PTA and the faculty are other ways leadership is exercised in the community, as are initiating and facilitating book clubs where community members read and meet to discuss the same book.

Other district-level teacher-leadership examples include:

Union Representative. The "union rep" is a teacher-leader who represents teacher interests, advises teachers who believe their rights have been infringed, and usually plays a role in negotiating contracts.

Professional Development Advocate. A teacher leads when he plans and/or facilitates professional development workshops to groups of colleagues. The professional development planning function usually involves working with other faculty, while facilitating/presenting is generally a solo endeavor.

TEACHERS LEAD BEYOND THEIR SCHOOL, DISTRICT, AND COMMUNITY

Some teacher-leaders opt to be part of their state's and nation's transformations and the rebuilding of teaching and learning. They want to feel as though their work improves students' lives and restores pride in and respect for the profession. As National Education Association President Dennis Van Roekel (2011) suggests, "[i]f we want to create an education system for the students of the 21st century, we must transform that system, including the teaching profession. Since teachers know best about what we do, teachers should take responsibility for leading the transformation of our profession."

Diana Beatty teaches math at a Colorado high school where her classroom is one of several located in the basement, which previously housed the cafeteria when the school was first built almost forty years ago. She educates students in the only basement classroom that has a window, but the window faces a brick wall. Her room is also not far from the school's noisy boiler room and a loading dock. When trucks arrive with deliveries, students are treated to loud rumblings that hijack their attention and cause the desks and chairs to vibrate. She has classes of 36 and 37 teenagers packed into desks that are falling apart, and students are using textbooks older than they are.

However, Beatty refused to let her students suffer in silence. She took her concerns directly to a national meeting which included NEA President Van Roekel, as well as education activists and stakeholders from across the country. The policy discussion focused on modernizing public schools nationwide, preventing hundreds of thousands of educator layoffs, and keeping students out of overcrowded classrooms.

Teacher-leaders have shared their passion by presenting at conferences. Others have written articles for educational journals or newsletters. For example, Lukwago (2011) writes about his belief that "schools become great when teachers share their knowledge and work in partnership with each other to facilitate the learning of all students." He describes in his college's newsletter that he decided to make a presentation on brain-based learning strategies available to his fellow teachers because he had observed how the strategies had helped his students get engaged and stay focused. Specifically, he described the use of music and movement to teach difficult concepts like the binary system and ASCII code for computer communications. Anderson and Nesholm (2010), Kelsey, Steel, and Steel (2002), Mayer (2011), Rupp-Fulwiler (2007, 2011), and Show and Woo (2008) are among many other teachers who have authored books based on their classroom experiences.

Blogging is another avenue teachers use to share their ideas, experiences, and suggestions. Schools Matter is a Web site that provides space for bloggers to explore issues in public education policy. For example, in a blog posted on Schools Matter, Thomas (2012) equates the dawning of the assembly line era of American manufacturing and its effect on the factory worker with where he suggests we now are heading in U.S. public education and its effect on the fate of the American teacher.

TEACHER-LEADER NETWORKS

Increasingly, teachers are becoming involved in affecting a wide range of education policy and practice. Some, like Colorado's Diana Beatty, are acting individually. Others are joining with colleagues in regional, state, and national networks of teacher-leaders.

In Kentucky, for example, a system of Leadership Networks has been developed to build and support the capacity of each district in the commonwealth as they implement Kentucky's new Core Academic Standards, develop assessment literacy among all educators, and work toward ensuring that every student is college and career ready. Participants in each of the Leadership Networks collaborate with other leaders throughout the region to hone practice and knowledge. The networks of mathematics teacher-leaders, English language arts (ELA) teacher-leaders, and school and district leaders held their first series of meetings in July 2010. About 2,500 teacher and district leaders throughout the state have participated in the process.

The Illinois New Millennium Initiative (NMI) core team is comprised of 14 teacher-leaders from across the state. Illinois passed a new teacher evaluation law in 2010, but the

NMI team has found that few teachers, principals, or school staff knew what is in the legislation or how it will affect them. The Illinois NMI teachers have developed materials to help educators and education officials understand the new law and the best practices for evaluation that should guide its implementation.

Other regional and state networks include members like Shanon C'de Baca, Lori Nazareno, and Marti Schwartz. Shanon is an online educator who not only brings her science knowledge and student-management skills to Iowa's virtual high school classrooms, but also trains new teachers via distance and face-to-face mentoring in Asia and the Middle East. Lori Nazareno coleads a Denver public school that's entirely run by teachers. In Rhode Island, Marti Schwartz mentors new teachers for Brown University, contracts privately to provide professional development in several community school systems, and also serves as a literacy teacher and coach at an inner-city high school.

A national network called The Teaching Policy Fellowship is a highly selective program for teachers interested in having a voice in decisions that affect their profession. During a cohort experience that spans 18 months, fellows meet in monthly sessions that offer:

- Personal interaction with key education leaders
- A challenging course of study in education policy, research, and best practices from across the nation
- The opportunity to advocate for policies that will better serve students and retain excellent teachers

Policy fellows are engaging in education reform in Boston, Chicago, Indianapolis, Los Angeles, and Memphis. Teaching policy fellows are all current classroom educators who teach a variety of subjects and grades, spanning from kindergarten through twelfth grade. Many fellows are also actively involved in their local teachers unions as building representatives and leadership committee members, and many are equally involved in school- or district-based leadership.

Teaching Policy fellows have influenced policy by participating in high-stakes national conferences and panels and publishing papers and articles. For example, Teaching Policy fellows have been invited to participate in NBC's nationally televised *Education Nation* to work with National Teacher Quality Advisor Brad Jupp on the redesign of the Elementary and Secondary Education Act, and to participate in the Gates Foundation's Measures of Effective Teaching panel. Teaching Policy fellows have been invited to present and to comment on new research at the Center for American Progress, the Vanderbilt National Center on Performance Incentives, and a meeting convened by New Leaders for New Schools and the Aspen Institute to counsel state leaders on their Race to the Top proposals.

The Teacher Leaders Network (TLN) is a highly active network of accomplished teachers engaged in diverse activities, such as mentoring novice and underprepared teachers, supporting National Board candidates, testing out lesson and assessment templates tied to the Common Core, engaging in policy conversations to advance teaching reforms, and working to transform unions into professional guilds. TLN members span all grades and school settings, from elementary teachers in urban neighborhoods of New York City to high school teachers in the rural Mississippi Delta. Twelve TLN members worked with the network's founder, Barnett Berry, in the writing of a book that paints a bold and hopeful vision for a 21st century results-oriented teaching profession (Berry, 2011b).

During his keynote address at the National Education Association's 2010 Representative Assembly in New Orleans, NEA President Dennis Van Roekel announced the formation of the Commission on Effective Teachers and Teaching (CETT). The commission draws on the wisdom and experience of 21 teacher-leaders supported by researchers, policymakers, and academicians who will examine the policies and practices governing the teaching profession and craft a new teacher-centered vision of teaching and the teaching profession. Chaired by Madaline "Maddie" Fennel, 2007 Nebraska Teacher of the Year and fourth-grade teacher from Omaha, Nebraska, CETT will meet four to six times during 2013 and conduct public hearings to gather input on topics of interest to the panel. Individual members of the commission will work on various committees and activities in order to deliver recommendations to the NEA Representative Assembly. NEA will use the recommendations to examine the Association's policies and long-term vision for teaching. See Appendix B for a list of the 21 original members of the Commission on Effective Teachers and Teaching.

In Summary

Teachers exhibit leadership in multiple, sometimes overlapping, ways. Some leadership roles are formal, with designated responsibilities. Other more informal roles emerge as teachers interact with their peers locally or are motivated to contribute to or influence some broader aspect of their profession. The wide variety of roles and opportunities ensures that teachers can find ways to lead that fit their talents and interests.

Teachers find many opportunities to lead within their own schools. They relate one-on-one in the classroom with colleagues as mentors, instructional or peer coaches, and modelers of lessons using research-based best practices. Outside the classroom, teacher-leaders address their school's policies and procedures by leading or participating in professional learning communities and departmental or interdisciplinary teams. Principal support—or lack thereof—will often determine whether such teams succeed. Principals who practice distributive leadership will let teachers know they recognize and look forward to teachers pooling their expertise to achieve the group's goal. Principals can also make data on the team's task available, and help staff members acquire skills needed to interpret data.

Extending beyond classrooms and school walls, teacher-leaders involve themselves in district-level issues as union representatives who advocate for teacher interests, as council members to offer advice to administration on key issues, as planners or presenters of district level professional development, or as leaders in the development of the district's core curriculum. Others express their leadership when they involve themselves in the local community by teaching adult education courses, speaking at school board meetings, or serving as a teacher liaison to the PTA.

Increasingly, teachers are expressing their leadership in educational issues beyond school, district, or community. They influence policy by participating in national conferences and panels and publishing papers and articles. They share their knowledge and experience by presenting at conferences. Others write articles for educational journals or newsletters.

Regardless of the roles they assume, teacher-leaders help shape the culture of their schools, districts, states, and nation. They influence the practice among their peers, impact the profession, and most importantly, work to improve student learning.

Chapter Discussion Questions

1. If you were the principal of a school and wanted to provide the opportunity for teachers to assume leadership roles, what are one or two things you would do to begin the process?

2. Effectively facilitating collaboration requires a teacher-leader to possess such collaborative skills as:
   - Promoting collaborative decision making
   - Engaging group members in team-building activities
   - Engaging group members in identifying and acknowledging problems
   - Recognizing and mediating conflict

   a. In your discussion group, develop a rubric for each of these four attributes.
   b. Based on the rubric the group created, assess and discuss the level of these collaboration skills within your group as you were engaged in the process of developing the rubric.

3. Should teachers have meaningful input into the school budget process? In selecting and/or evaluating administrators and teachers? If not, why not? If so, what should these processes entail?

CHAPTER

6

Learning to Lead

Teachers need training to become effective leaders. How do you run a meeting? How do you ask great questions to further the learning of colleagues? How do you give feedback to your colleagues? We have to be intentional in our development of [teacher-leaders] because I would assert that teachers don't come to teaching with that knowledge.

—PHYLLIS PAJARDO (2011), ASSISTANT SUPERINTENDENT, FAIRFAX COUNTY, VA

This chapter examines the skills, understandings, and competencies that characterize an effective teacher-leader, and where and how those attributes are acquired, used, and enhanced. Experienced teachers take on the challenge and responsibility of leadership with high hopes, good intentions, and—generally—a natural charisma. Classroom expertise, hope, good intentions, and a winning smile, however, will not by themselves guarantee effective and accomplished performance as a teacher-leader. A dedicated, experienced teacher of children may have little experience or limited patience for working with adults. They may not be skilled in making public presentations, facilitating workshops, or serving as agents of change.

In a study of teacher-leaders in the Vesta, Georgia School District, Kelley (2011) found that only one of nine teacher-leaders had formal training concerning teacher leadership skill sets. One teacher stated that teachers, including some formal teacher-leaders who serve as mentors, have received district training in mentoring, but most ". . . kind of like just jump [sic] in the water and learned how to swim" (p. 150). Another teacher-leader observed that training was not offered, and that administrators based selection for the role in part on what type of related training they may have had.

When in the position to lead, whether it is leading other individuals or school or district teams, even when those individuals or teams have energy and enthusiasm, leaders require the skills, tools, and support structures that would allow them to orchestrate significant peda-gogical and curriculum changes. Team leaders, for example, are rarely if ever trained in even the basic skills of team facilitation such as time management, goal setting, develop-ment of team norms, and conflict resolution. Preparing highly skilled classroom teachers to be effective teacher-leaders takes training as well as a system of support (Troen & Boles, 2011a).

What it boils down to is that in order for teacher leadership roles to successfully ful-fill their intended purpose, the teachers who have assumed these roles must be able to perform them well. This generally requires mastery of a repertoire of leadership skills that lie far beyond those required for effective classroom practice. The question is, what consti-tutes the knowledge, skills, and competencies that teachers need in order to assume lead-ership roles in their schools and districts in particular, and in the profession in general?

TEACHER-LEADER STANDARDS

In May 2008, a group of concerned educators convened to examine the current research and thoughts on the critical leadership roles that teachers play, and to explore opportuni-ties to provide meaningful positions for teacher-leaders in the nation's schools. The con-sortium was particularly focused on teachers who seek leadership roles, but do not want to leave the classroom. This initial group subsequently expanded its membership and mission to form the Teacher Leadership Exploratory Consortium (Appendix C) that repre-sents a broad array of education organizations, state education agencies, teacher-leaders, principals, superintendents, and institutions of higher education. The consortium's efforts ultimately focused on identifying what constitutes the knowledge, skills, and competen-cies that teachers need to assume teacher leadership roles in their schools, districts, and the profession. The results of their work resulted in the development and publication of its Model Standards for Teacher Leadership (2011) (Appendix D), a set of standards mod-eled on the Interstate School Leaders Licensure Consortium (ISLLC) State Standards for School Leaders (1996).

The Teacher Leadership Exploratory Consortium's standards describe the skills, knowledge, and competencies that teachers need to perform well in leadership roles. The standards are laid out as a series of seven broadly stated domains that identify critical dimensions of teacher leadership.

> Domain I: Fostering a collaborative culture to support educator development and student learning
>
> Domain II: Accessing and using research to improve practice and student learning
>
> Domain III: Promoting professional learning for continuous improvement
>
> Domain IV: Facilitating improvements in instruction and student learning
>
> Domain V: Promoting the use of assessments and data for school and district improvement
>
> Domain VI: Improving outreach and collaboration with families and community
>
> Domain VII: Facilitating improvements in instruction and student learning

Each domain includes functions that further define the scope of actions or expectations related to that domain.

Hirsh (2011) believes that these standards "will guide the development of future teacher leaders and provide current teacher leaders with a benchmark for assessing their leadership expertise. The standards provide a framework for the professional development teacher leaders need to be effective in their roles and to prepare them to facilitate professional learning among their colleagues." The standards are increasingly being used for curriculum for higher education coursework, establishing teacher-leader roles in schools, drafting legislation and state-specific standards, and planning professional development for both teachers and school leaders.

LEADERSHIP DEVELOPMENT PROGRAMS

An increasing number of educational organizations at local, regional, and state levels are providing professional development opportunities and creating academic courses for teacher-leaders. What these organizations include in their programs present a litany of the knowledge, skills, and behaviors they consider important for aspiring teacher-leaders.

The Boston Teacher Leadership Resource Center (TLRC), established in partnership with the Boston Public Schools, the Boston Plan for Excellence, and the Boston Teacher Residency Program, is an example of such an initiative. The TLRC series of courses were designed by teacher-leaders. Participants have the option of earning three graduate credits from Cambridge College or from UMass Boston's CAGS program in teacher leadership. Teachers who complete each of the core courses earn the Boston Teacher Leadership Certificate, distinguishing them as professionals with leadership expertise. The TLRC courses include:

- *Using Data*—Participants learn how to access and collect multiple forms of data and build a repertoire of strategies for guiding their teams to understand, analyze, and use data in decision-making and to communicate data results in ways that empower community members to envision their role in improvement.
- *Supporting Instruction*—Participants gain expertise in applying principles of adult learning as they learn and practice strategies for observing teaching, examining student work collaboratively, analyzing instruction and instructional resources, facilitating growth-oriented dialogue, and planning effective professional learning experiences.
- *Shared Leadership*—Participants learn approaches for building unity of vision within a team, managing an effective, collaborative team, facilitating change, and understanding the role of individuals and teams within school and district systems.
- *Professional Expertise*—Participants build routines for guiding team reflection and harnessing professional expertise within a school, while also building skills to access and use the professional knowledge base and to apply that knowledge to systemic improvement.

Concordia University in Chicago offers an online doctoral program in teacher leadership. The program's courses reflect what are generally considered to be some of the core underpinnings of teacher leadership. They include:

- Instructional Leadership
- Organizational Change
- Adult Learning
- Philosophical and Theoretical Foundations of Leadership

- Assessment, Evaluation, and Data-Driven Decision Making
- Instructional Coaching for Effective Teaching
- Ethics for Educational Leaders
- Curriculum Theory and Design
- Building Collaborative Relationships
- Policy Analysis
- Influencing the School Culture
- Providing Instructional Support
- Leading School-Based Professional Learning Communities
- Research-Based Decision Making

The Leadership Institute of Riverside County (LIRC) at the Riverside County Office of Education (2012) is designed to acknowledge and validate the contributions of the county's experienced and exceptional teacher-leaders. The activities leading to the certificate are based on the Teacher Leadership Exploratory Consortium's Teacher Leadership Standards and are designed to:

- Foster a collaborative culture to support educator development and student learning
- Access and use research to improve practice and student achievement
- Promote professional learning for continuous improvement
- Facilitate improvements in instruction and student learning
- Use assessments and data for school and district improvement
- Improve outreach and collaboration with families and community
- Advocate for student learning and the profession

Upon successful completion of the program requirements, candidates receive recommendation for Teacher Leaders Certification by LIRC.

Penn State has launched a 30-credit distance education program—an online M.Ed. in Educational Leadership with an option in Teacher Leadership. The program is organized around five strands of teacher leadership: responsible influence, understanding internal organization of schools, ongoing professional development, powerful curriculum and instruction practices, and practice-based inquiry.

The Aspen Institute, headquartered in Washington, D.C., conducts the Aspen Teacher Leader Fellows Program that is designed to cultivate and support cohorts of teacher-leaders. The program's seminars feature thought-provoking reading and discussions about leadership, diversity, and important issues in public education and social change. In addition, fellows design and undertake projects aimed at strengthening the teaching profession and the capacity of educators to improve student achievement. When they complete the program, fellows become part of the Aspen Global Leadership Network, which includes nearly 1400 entrepreneurial leaders from 43 countries who share a commitment to educational leadership.

The Philadelphia Education Fund sponsors a monthly forum for teachers focusing on teacher leadership. The forum considers how teacher leadership can support effective curricula, instruction, assessment, and policy. Shared readings and guest speakers provide a context and guide discussions. Questions considered include:

- What does it mean to be a teacher-leader?
- How can teacher leadership enrich learning environments?
- How can school communities sustain teacher leadership?

The initial sessions were facilitated by teacher-leader Gamal Sherif, a science and history teacher with the School District of Philadelphia. In addition to his teaching responsibilities, Gamal served as a Teaching Ambassador Fellow with the U.S. Department of Education, and has participated in the Center for Teaching Quality's Teacher Leaders Network.

In Manchester in the United Kingdom, Teaching Leaders is an initiative designed to measurably raise levels of pupil achievement in what are determined to be challenging schools by training a cadre of middle leaders consisting of heads of department, heads of year, and other whole-school roles. Teaching Leaders was developed in partnership with four U.K. educational organizations: Absolute Return for Kids (ARK), the National College, Teach First, and Future Leaders. The program provides training over a 2-year period in a wide variety of management and leadership areas such as delegation, creating a positive and open working climate, team building, developing political intelligence, negotiation and influence, and managing change.

In the private sector, several organizations rely on their own managers and administrators to conduct leadership teaching sessions. According to a blog posted by Lamoureax (2009), executives at aircraft manufacturer Textron teach modules of senior level programs to other employees, and at Telecommunications Systems Inc., executives have to *apply* to teach leadership programs. Cohen and Tichy (1997) describe how former General Electric CEO Jack Welch conducted leadership sessions every couple of weeks, and that Intel requires its top personnel to teach leadership sessions. Schools and districts would do well to emulate business and industry by creating a culture where people teach each other.

STATE LICENSE ENDORSEMENTS RECOGNIZE TEACHER LEADERSHIP

Like a growing number of other teachers nationwide, Danna S. Clinton, a 27-year veteran physics teacher at the 2,400-student Lafayette High School in Lafayette, Louisiana has taken on a variety of leadership roles in her school, from chairing the science department to helping with the school's improvement plan. But she has one thing many of her colleagues do not have: a teacher leadership endorsement from the state of Louisiana testifying to her skills. Louisiana, Illinois, Georgia, Delaware, and Kentucky are among several states that have created or are considering adding endorsements to their state licensing systems that would formally recognize teachers who complete coursework in teacher leadership, and who then implement school reform, revise instructional programs, coach fellow teachers, foster a school environment conducive to learning, or assume other nonadministrative leadership tasks or leadership roles outside their own classrooms (Olson, 2007).

The actual requirements for the endorsements, which recognize a specific area of expertise on top of the basic license required to become a teacher, vary across states. In Louisiana, for instance, teacher-leaders must complete 6 hours of graduate coursework in educational leadership that can also be used toward a master's degree. In Illinois, teachers can earn the endorsement by completing a master's program in teacher leadership, but those in the state who are certified by the National Board for Professional Teaching Standards or who have already demonstrated leadership experience in their schools can complete a smaller sequence of courses. In Georgia, the endorsement programs must address a variety of leadership functions, including how to develop and implement a shared school vision, provide effective instructional programs based on Georgia standards, and design comprehensive professional-growth plans for adults. Acquiring a teacher-leader endorsement is a key step in securing Ohio's new Lead Professional Educator license. This endorsement is based on Ohio's Teacher Leader (OTL) Standards. The OTL standards promote a comprehensive set of teacher leadership competencies, including: 1) Assisting administrative leaders in developing and supporting a shared educational vision for 21st-century learning 2) Managing the conflict and tensions that accompany 21st-century educational reform 3) Facilitating continuous adult learning through collaborative inquiry formats 4) Functioning as peer coaches and mentors with teaching colleagues at all stages of their careers.

The New Jersey Education Association proposed creating a Teacher Leader endorsement on the state's standard instructional certificate that would "codify the skills, knowledge, and requirements necessary to fulfill that role, and allow districts to recognize and reward those who are qualified to lead and choose to do so. Requirements would be high, and only experienced educators who intentionally pursue additional education and training would qualify to earn the endorsement" (NJEA Review, 2011, p. 11).

One thing is true across all the states so far: The endorsements are purely optional. Teachers don't need to hold an endorsement to assume leadership roles in their schools. And the endorsements do not assure a teacher of any extra pay, unless a district chooses to provide it, although local bargaining agreements may consider the credential to mark teachers for salary increases, perhaps as part of career-ladder systems.

MENTORING FUTURE TEACHER-LEADERS

Teacher-leaders can help develop future leaders by encouraging and coaching colleagues to serve as backups to their positions. A teacher leading a professional learning community, for example, might sit down with an interested committee member, explain the nature of the role, and discuss details involved in preparing for a meeting. After a meeting, the two can meet and discuss the details of the facilitator's actions and their results. In addition to a teacher-leader helping a colleague acquire essential leadership skills and knowledge in order to train a backup or even her successor for when she moves on, the colleague will be better prepared to take on a leadership role elsewhere.

In Summary

Teachers who assume the role of teacher-leader must possess a mastery of leadership skills that lie far beyond those required for effective classroom practice. The Teacher Leadership Exploratory Consortium, representing state education agencies, teacher-leaders, principals, superintendents, and institutions of higher education, identified the knowledge, skills, and competencies that teachers need to assume teacher leadership roles in their schools, districts, and professions. The Consortium's deliberations resulted in The Model Standards for Teacher Leadership. The standards are laid out as a series of seven broadly stated domains, each further defined by a set of functions that describe the skills, knowledge, and competencies that teachers need to perform well in leadership roles.

In recognition of the growing number of teacher-leader roles in education and the importance of leadership skills and competencies to the effective implementation of those roles, increasing numbers of school districts, professional associations, and institutions of higher education have designed and are offering leadership training programs to teachers. Several states have created or are considering adding endorsements to their state licensing systems that would formally recognize teachers who complete programs in teacher leadership.

Chapter Discussion Questions

Domain I of the Model Standard for Teacher Leadership—fostering a collaborative culture to support educator development and student learning—begins with the statement, "The teacher leader is well versed in adult learning theory and uses that knowledge to create a community of collective responsibility within his or her school."

1. What are the principles of adult learning?
2. How might a teacher-leader go about building collegiality, trust, and respect in a group where all the individuals are focused on continuous improvement in instruction and student learning?
3. What observable measurable behaviors might one see and hear as a group works together as colleagues?
4. What functions in the standards inform your responses to the above questions?

SECTION III

The Leader of Leader Culture

Chapter 7   Shaping School Culture: We Don't Know What We Don't Know
Chapter 8   School Climate and Culture
Chapter 9   Building Sustainability

CHAPTER

7 Shaping School Culture
We Don't Know What We Don't Know

There are known knowns; there are things we know that we know. There are known unknowns; that is to say, there are things that we know we don't know. But there are also unknown unknowns—there are things we do not know we don't know.

—Donald Rumsfeld, 2002

Taking up the principalship at a new school, whether for the veteran administrator or the newbie, is a unique experience. While there are certainly many commonalities among schools, there is something unique about every school that the arriving principal cannot know. Each new principalship is in some way a leap of faith, stepping into that which must be experienced to be known. The good news is that those who do possess an intimate knowledge of the school surround the new principal. We are speaking, of course, of the teachers. Danielson (2007) contends that "teachers often hold the institutional memory; they are the custodians of the school culture" (p. 18).

While each teacher might not possess the "big picture" perspective that the principal needs, taken collectively they almost certainly have enough pieces of the puzzle. The question for the principal is how he or she will approach that puzzle. It has been our experience that there exists with most school leaders a reluctance to share leadership for fear of being seen as weak. Many new principals fake it until they make it—or, unfortunately, don't make it—without enlisting the teachers in their mission.

"US" AND "THEM" MENTALITY

This chapter postulates that if principals don't collaborate with teachers to create the school's culture, the school's culture will create itself. There is a prevalence of an "us" versus "them"— mentality between administrators and teachers. It is not odd that this approach is adopted so frequently in school systems with a hierarchical leadership structure. It is frequently the administrators who are the variable while the teachers are the constant. In other words, the institutional history and continuity rest with the teachers, who see many principals come and go over the course of their teaching careers. What *is* odd is that principals do not tap into that wealth of collective institutional knowledge more often, or actively enlist the help of those who are invested in sticking around for the long term.

As principals come and go, each trying to distinguish her or his leadership from that of their predecessor, rules and procedures are interpreted according to the personal vision of the school's current leader. Teachers adapt and do what needs to be done to outwardly please each subsequent new boss, but it is rarer that the principal works to create a genuinely shared vision. The most ironic aspect of this situation is that a common vision is what would ultimately bring about the elusive sustainable change that principals seek.

Johnson and Donaldson (2007) found that emergent teacher-leaders struggle against the traditional norms of teaching, which include "autonomy, egalitarianism, and seniority" (p. 13). These norms "reinforce the privacy of the individual's classroom, limit the exchange of good ideas among colleagues, and suppress efforts to recognize expert teaching [by exerting] a powerful and persistent influence on the work of teachers [that ultimately caps] a school's instructional quality far below its potential" (p. 13).

Newton's first law of motion tells us that a body will remain in uniform motion unless acted upon by an equal and opposite force. Principals are that force. Principals can counter teacher tendency to stay in the classroom. The decades of teachers as independent subcontractors are over. No longer can a principal hand the newly hired teacher keys to his or her classroom, maybe pop into the classroom three times a year to conduct an observation, and still have the slightest expectation that professional growth or teacher leadership will be fostered.

The opportunity to make a difference attracts many teachers to choose to become leaders, yet their path to teacher leadership is hindered by lingering myths about leadership. The first myth is that there can only be a single leader in the school—the principal— and all others are followers. The second myth is that teachers cannot simultaneously be teacher-leaders and classroom teachers; teachers must choose to give up the teaching they love to step into a leadership role. Because of these myths, Some potential teacher-leaders never realize the myriad ways teachers and their students benefit from teachers taking on leadership roles (Somnath, Hanuscin, Rebello, Muslu, & Cheng, 2012).

Principals are in a position to dispel the myths held by potential teacher-leaders and, by doing so, change the leadership trajectory of potential teacher-leaders. This is somewhat self-serving; encouraging teacher-leaders helps the principal and the school. "As teachers commit to shared outcomes, they are able to influence both practice and change in their schools and become involved in assuming leadership. It is when teachers lead that schools become places where all members of the learning community benefit" (Kadela, 2009, p. 9). Wade and Ferriter (2007) tell the story of Carolann. This teacher-leader reflected on how she was hesitant to pursue a leadership role until the support and encouragement of an administrator caused her to take that first step. "I often wonder how my career would have been different had that district administrator not personally invited me to lead. Like many classroom teachers, I was unaware of the array of leadership opportunities available to educators" (p. 67).

Danielson (2006) declares, "[e]nlightened administrators recognize that achieving their aims of high-level student learning can happen only through the active engagement of teacher leaders. Thus, even if they were not committed to teacher leadership, self-interest would suggest that cultivation of teacher leaders is a wise move" (p. 126). Principals need to evolve and, to use Danielson's term, become enlightened. Principals moving schools forward is not just about leadership, it is about *enlightened* leadership. Enlightened principals encourage fledging teacher-leaders to step out of their comfort zone and take a risk. This may require principals to step outside of their own comfort zone as well; sharing leadership can be scary if it is a new experience or was unsuccessfully attempted in the past.

Ackerman and Mackenzie (2006) speak to the catch-22 of developing teacher leadership. "The rub for all teacher leaders? Their strength comes from the classroom, yet unless they venture out of it, connecting and relating to other adults in the school, they do not fulfill the power implicit in their teaching role" (p. 66). Principals can face what they perceive as their own catch-22. If principals perceive that strength in leadership equates with one person calling all the shots and managing everything, then the thought of distributive leadership and collaborative decision making can only be seen as making the principal less of a leader. The irony is that enlightened school leaders who foster strong teacher leadership actually make themselves more of a leader, not less.

It is important that principals be the first risk takers in their schools, if they expect others to follow suit. Glover (2007) calls upon principals to create a safe climate that promotes risk taking. He states that "real leadership challenges the leader before it challenges others" (p. 63). Perceived helplessness, whether on the part of the principal or the teacher, can be pervasive and immobilize a school. Federal mandates such as No Child Left Behind and Race to the Top, as well as individual state mandates, have convinced many educators that they are helpless. Principals can choose to validate this sense of helplessness or allow teachers to have a voice in the decisions impacting their school. Glover calls on principals who lead in a climate "thick with education mandates" (p. 60) to recognize that many teachers fear that "their chances to influence decisions about their profession are eroding. Principals must find ways to change that perception so that teachers see that, at least in their own schools, their voices are heard and their risk taking makes a difference" (p. 60).

HEROES NEED NOT APPLY

The time has come to dispel the myth of the great man/woman theory of leadership. Crevani, Lindgren, and Packendorff (2010) suggest delimiting leadership practices and interactions in the emergence of this new leadership era. Schools are moving beyond a "postheroic leadership ideals" (p. 78) era. Modern leaders "emphasize the relational, collectivist, and non-authoritarian nature of leadership practices in contemporary organizations" (p. 78). Few teacher-leaders can thrive under an authoritarian principal.

There is a good reason that principals are not issued a cape and tights when they assume the principalship: Schools are not led by superheroes. Spillane (2005) speaks of the fallacy of the notion of the "heroics of leadership," where one charismatic principal is going to swoop in, take care of all the school's problems, and transform the school's culture single-handedly. A study by Margolis and Deuel (2009) that closely examined the teacher leadership of five teachers concluded that "[i]f we are to truly transform teaching, learning, and schools, then we need to look closely at the structures (both economic and emotional) that support teacher leadership as a way to build capacity for sustained change efforts" (p. 282).

The problem with a heroic view of leadership, as Spillane points out, is twofold.

One, schools are not led to greatness by the efforts of one individual; "[L]eadership involves an array of individuals with various tools and structures" (p. 143). Two, thinking only about the "what" of leadership and not the "how" of leadership is misguided. We must begin to frame our understanding of leadership more contextually. Leadership is not a series of tasks to be checked off of a list, but rather, an ongoing process. It is time for the heroic view to be reframed; principals need to turn their attention to the process of leading, or the "how" of leadership.

Sydow, Lerch, Huxham, and Hibbert (2011) offer a "structuration" perspective of leadership. Sydow et al. suggest that "leadership, like any action, necessarily relies on structures (including relationships) that are produced and reproduced—and eventually transformed—by the very action that 'makes things happen'" (p. 10). The aim for principals is to use existing or build new structures: to be transformational leaders as opposed to transactional leaders. Bass (1990) characterizes transactional leaders as only intervening when standards are not met, as compared to the transformational leader's approach, which is characterized by individualized attention, advice, and coaching to followers. Teacher-leaders need the latter style of leadership.

TRANSFORMATIONAL VERSUS TRANSACTIONAL LEADERSHIP

The transactional leader is someone "who promises rewards for good performance," while the transformational leader is someone who provides "vision and sense of mission, instills pride, gains respect and trust" (Bass, 1990, p. 22). "Transformational leaders act as mentors to their followers by encouraging learning, achievement, and individual development. They provide meaning, act as role models, provide challenges, evoke emotions, and foster a climate of trust" (Harms & Credé, 2010, p. 6).

Bass (1990) distinguishes the transformational leader from the transactional leader by the leader's impact on making the work they do meaningful for followers. Teachers will not willingly step into teacher-leader roles when they cannot find meaning in doing so. Yukl (1999) defined intellectual stimulation as "causing a subordinate to question traditional beliefs, to look at problems in a different way, and to find innovative solutions for problems" (pp. 288–289).

Bass found it essential for leaders to position themselves to think systemically and view the big picture if they hoped to bring about transformation in their organizations. Leaders and, we would argue, teacher-leaders, "whose jobs force them to focus on solving small, immediate problems are likely to be less intellectually stimulated than those who have time to think ahead and in larger terms" (Bass, 1990, p. 30). The idea is that leaders can transform an organization by motivating those who follow to achieve a higher level of consciousness, so that organizational goals supersede self-interest. Bass identifies leadership as falling along a continuum (Figure 7.1) rather than in completely separate stages. Leaders are not pigeonholed to operate exclusively from one mode of leadership: the negative form of leadership—laissez-faire; the more positive form—transactional leadership; or the highest form of leadership—transformational. Leaders may be operating

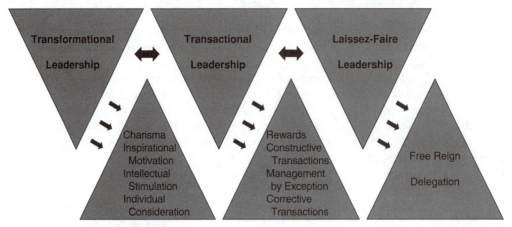

FIGURE 7.1 Leadership Continuum

from anywhere along the continuum; it is not uncommon for leaders to practice a multi-modal leadership approach. The more transformational the leadership approach, the more connections are made, altering followers' motivations beyond simple punishment, contingent rewards, and management by exception (Burns, 1978). While transformational leadership raises the level of engagement between leader and follower, this increased connection between leader and follower also alters the leader's motivation.

TEACHER-LEADER LITE

No doubt many principals could tick off a long list of perceived teacher-leaders in their school if asked "Who are the teacher-leaders in your school?" We would argue that many of these teacher-leader roles are in actuality "teacher-leader lite" or leader-plus positions and not genuine leadership roles. A culture of teacher leadership moves beyond teachers being considered teacher-leaders merely because they were assigned, or volunteered for, a role outside the classroom. Assuming such a role does not mean that the teacher is not a teacher-leader, simply that teacher roles outside of the classroom are not synonymous with teacher leadership. The difference is that teacher-leaders share in the leadership; they are part of constructing the process, not merely managing an event or process created by someone else, most likely the principal. If lite beer is less filling, than teacher-leader lite is less fulfilling.

Spillane (2005) warned of confusing what he referred to as "leader plus" with the genuine distribution of leadership. Simply identifying leader helpers is not synonymous with distributing leadership "over an interactive web of people and situations, examining how leadership is spread over both leaders and followers . . ." (p. 144). Leadership is interpersonal. Spillane suggests three reasons why "equating leadership with the actions of those in leadership positions is inadequate" (p. 145).

1. Leadership typically involves more than one leader, including those with and without formal positions of leadership.
2. Leadership is not "done to" followers, but is defined by the actions of others.
3. The critical practices in leadership are the interactions among individuals, not the actions of individuals.

The principals can intensify the commitment of teacher-leaders by increasing their level of commitment. Hulpia, Devos, and Van Keer (2011) found that school leaders need to be "aware that teachers' organizational commitment is influenced by teachers' opportunity to participate in school decision making . . . [and] when teachers are offered a chance to participate in decision-making processes, their organizational commitment is intensified" (p. 759).

PRINCIPAL ROBERTA LAYS THE FOUNDATION FOR A SCHOOL CULTURE

When Roberta first arrived at the Sorrin School, the principal's office had been somewhat of a revolving door. Even some of the youngest teachers had worked with a number of principals before her. The frequency of changes in the principalship presented a virtue and a vice all in one. On the one hand, the faculty and staff were accustomed to a high degree of autonomy that comes from inconsistent leadership, making the ground fertile to foster teacher-leaders. On the other hand, the faculty and staff were so accustomed to making things run without consistent leadership that there was resistance to make changes for yet another short-timer principal.

Roberta's arrival, seen as yet another in a long string of principals by the majority of the faculty, was a case of once bitten, twice shy. The name on the school letterhead changed frequently, but there was a sense among the teachers, and with good reason, that getting invested in yet another short-timer's vision for the school would be a waste of time and energy. The faculty had witnessed too many short-tenured principals come and go to think this time would be any different. Most of the teachers figured they could hold their breath longer than the time any new initiative Roberta would propose could last. Being the latest in a long line of instructional leaders presented a leadership challenge. Roberta knew she had to take a different approach to leading this school. At the first faculty meeting, Roberta set out to accomplish two things: demand failure and seek the teachers' advice.

DEMANDING FAILURE

Demanding failure seems counterintuitive to what schools are all about, but it is actually where schools get hung up. Not accepting mistakes as an integral part of learning results in teachers ceasing to try to improve their practice for fear of failing. The message needs to be that it is okay for everyone to make mistakes, as long as we use them to learn and improve. How can teachers—or students, for that matter—be challenged to think outside the box and take appropriate risks, if simultaneously they are not given permission to fail? The permission to fail cannot be left for the teachers to infer; the principal has to explicitly state, "You will fail from time to time on the road to improving your instruction. As the one who evaluates your performance, I am not only okay with you experiencing failures, I expect it. If you are not making mistakes, I will be concerned that you are not on the road to improving your instruction!"

Roberta recognized the culture that is generated when failure is a high-stakes proposition: a culture of playing it safe. What employees will try something new if they think their boss is going to penalize them if a daring new idea is unsuccessful? Conversely, children's time in each grade is limited and needs to be spent judiciously; it is unacceptable for teachers to take inappropriate risks that squander valuable time students cannot afford to lose with mistake after instructional mistake.

Roberta made it a point to make a distinction between good mistakes—those that come about as the result of taking an appropriate risk—and repeated mistakes—those that squander precious instructional time. If a teacher exemplifies an *appropriate* risks model of a safe educational environment, it serves as a model for her students. When the teacher can say to the students in his class, "We are trying something today in which I am not sure of the outcome, but I think there is a good deal to be learned from trying it," it speaks volumes to the students about appropriate risk taking as a an integral part of a healthy learning environment.

PRINCIPAL ROBERTA SHARES HER HARE-BRAINED THEORY

Roberta told her staff that everyone should consider developing a theory. As an example at that first meeting, Roberta shared her theory on brilliant ideas with the faculty. She told the members of the faculty to envision a pyramid. She had them imagine that the bottom third of the pyramid was filled with 1,000 absolutely hare-brained ideas. Those 1,000 hare-brained ideas would generate about 100 plausible ideas, which would fill the middle third of the pyramid. Ten good ideas would rise up to occupy the top third of the pyramid. On the very pinnacle of the pyramid would stand one brilliant idea.

The point of Roberta's theory is not to produce a scientific formula showing that for every 1,000 hare-brained ideas one brilliant idea emerges, but instead it's designed to liberate teachers from a stifling environment where teachers can only put forth brilliant ideas (Figure 7.2). That is not how creativity works. In school it needs to be okay to think outside the box, even if those thoughts will not become brilliant ideas. It needs to be okay to brainstorm; it needs to be acceptable to put forth less than fully developed notions. Oftentimes, someone picks up the pieces of a failed idea and builds upon it. It is

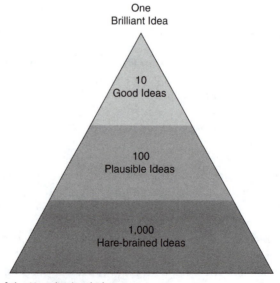

FIGURE 7.2 Theory of the Hare-brained Ideas

difficult to realize the synergy of collaboration if one has to worry about putting forth only perfectly polished ideas.

In the second part of that first faculty meeting, Roberta sought the teachers' advice in identifying the strengths and challenges facing the school through a simple mini needs assessment. Each teacher was handed a white index card. She instructed them to anonymously write down three things of which they were most proud about their school on one side, and on the other side, the "B-side," the three things that they perceived to be the biggest challenges facing the school. This primitive needs assessment was instrumental in all of the successes that followed.

This needs assessment did not just take the pulse of the faculty. In her first face-to-face interaction with the faculty, it stated that as their new principal Roberta wanted to know teachers' opinions. Asking teachers to share their thoughts recognized and reinforced that teachers are the constant, while she, as the administrator, was the variable in the equation.

The next step was critical. This point is worth repeating: *The next step was critical.* Something actually had to be done with the information collected on the cards. If no connection was made between what was written on what would later become known as "the white cards" and Roberta's first 100 days as principal, it would have been detrimental to the faculty's trust in the possibility that things could be different.

At the following faculty meeting, Roberta shared what the faculty was proud about and what they perceived as challenges. Their individual notions were sorted into common themes; this was the beginning of a shared vision (and it was only the second faculty meeting). Once articulated, Roberta immediately began looking for what Schmoker (2006b) refers to as the "small wins."

SMALL WINS

Roberta only later found out that Schmoker had a name for what she was doing. Schmoker characterized what she was doing as using "small wins," the most powerful lever to overcome resistance and promote buy-in on the road to improving morale and effective practice. Roberta began instituting small wins by picking the low-hanging fruit, by addressing the relatively easy challenges, and by building slowly to the more complex issues. Whenever a challenge from the "B-side" of the white cards was tackled, whether big or small, it was immediately disseminated to the school community with the footnote that it was a white card challenge.

That whole first year and into the middle of her second year, Roberta concentrated on ticking off white card concerns. Halfway through her second year, a sufficient number of white card challenges had been tackled to cause teachers to dare to consider the possibility that what they dreamed for their school could become a reality. The issues addressed in those first 18 months were not hers; they belonged exclusively to the teachers. Roberta was carrying out *their* visions. The only major exception to carrying out teacher-inspired initiatives was the establishment of a new teacher induction and mentoring program.

Together, Roberta and the teachers hired an additional custodian and began to build a collective sense of pride in the appearance of their school. Prior to Roberta's arrival, the parent teacher organization (PTO) held fundraisers to pay a small stipend to staff the library part-time. Restoring the library with a full-time librarian was a big deal to the classroom teachers, who saw library time as vital to the mission of an elementary school. Roberta worked with the district business manager to reprioritize funds and reopen the library fulltime.

Once small ideas are repeatedly seen to transform into realities, more teachers dare to think that their bigger ideas might become realities too. Once bigger ideas are transformed into realities, teachers begin to believe that they can shape the reality around them. When those in a school believe that they have a voice in translating ideas, both big and small, into realities, then the reshaping of a school's culture has begun.

TRUST BUILDING

Trust between the principal and the teacher-leaders, and trust among teacher-leaders have to exist for a strong foundation upon which to cultivate a school culture of teacher leadership. Blase and Blase (2002) suggest that now, more than any other time in history, school reform "require[s] that principals and teachers at the school level work together collaboratively to solve educational problems" (p. 721). They suggest that for principal and teacher collaboration to be successful, principals must build trust in their schools. This trust, "in turn, serves as a foundation for open, honest, and reflective professional dialogue; problem solving; innovative initiatives; and more directly, the development of the school as a powerful community of learners willing to take responsibility for and capable of success" (p. 721).

Năstase (2010) states that while trust is important, it needs to be seen as a means to an end. "Personal trust and enthusiasm can represent important variables in implementing the leaders' vision and reaching the strategic objectives" (p. 457); however, the leader articulates a common vision. "The staff, even if it trusts the leaders, is more and more eager to know their vision, to understand the objectives that are followed and what its role is in the organizational mechanism" (p. 457). Both personal trust for the principal and a school culture of trust are integral to fostering teacher-leaders.

SITUATIONAL AWARENESS

The modern principal often faces more responsibilities than there are hours in the workday, leaving the principal to prioritize tasks. This is one of the reasons that teacher-leaders are essential to bringing order to the complexity of modern schools. The modern principal may be asking, "With so many demands competing for my attention, on what should I, the over-burdened principal, concentrate my attention?" As mentioned in Chapter 1, one of the most in-depth analyses on the impact of leadership as it relates to student achievement was performed by Marzano, Waters, and McNulty (2005). Marzano and his colleagues found that out of 21 school leader responsibilities, the strongest relationship between principal responsibility and student achievement was linked to situational awareness.

While situational awareness may not be a principal's panacea, it is essential to both student achievement and to influencing school culture. In respect to fostering teacher-leaders, situational awareness is key. The principal needs to understand the subtleties and undercurrents of the school. This allows the principal to know which teacher-leaders are meeting with resistance, who is ready to be nudged toward taking on a teacher-leadership role, and who needs more time before taking on the challenges of becoming a teacher-leader.

It is important that principals do not confuse situational awareness with effective teacher observations. There needs to be a distinction between "popping in" to a classroom and the intentionality of focused classroom visits that have the "explicit purpose of engaging with teachers about well-defined instructional ideas and issues" (Louis, Leithwood, Wahlstrom, & Anderson, 2010, pp. 90–91).

In a 2010 Wallace Foundation report on the links to improved student learning, Louis et al. discovered that principals "do not lose influence as others gain it. Influence does not come in fixed quantities. Influential leaders wishing to retain their influence may share leadership confidently" (Louis, Leithwood, Wahlstrom, & Anderson, 2010, pp. 282–283). There is no "single best way to distribute or share leadership" (p. 282), but "when principals and teachers share leadership, teachers' working relationships with one another were stronger and student achievement was higher" (p. 282). The report suggested that teachers were more likely to employ instructional practices linked to improving learning when they felt that they were a part of a professional community of shared leadership.

ONE DEGREE MAKES ALL THE DIFFERENCE

What is "the difference"? The difference all schools seek is to improve student outcomes. How schools define outcomes may differ. It is hoped that improving student outcomes does not simply mean improving student test scores, but rather improving students' experiences as well as their opportunities beyond school. There exists an ethical onus on principals, teacher-leaders, and teachers alike to treat fairly those students entrusted to their care.

Ultimately, "the difference" is achieved through building school capacity. Cosner (2009) defines school capacity as "comprised of a collection of organizational resources, interactive in nature, that supports school wide reform work, teacher change, and ultimately the improvement of student learning" (p. 250).

Building school capacity depends upon teacher cooperation. Teacher cooperation depends upon the principal building trust. Trust impacts every interaction within a school, "whether interactions are between individuals, within teams or subgroups, or among an entire staff" (Cosner, 2009, p. 251), without trust uncertainty prevails.

There is a veteran elementary principal who has a motivational poster hanging in her office. This poster speaks about the difference one degree can make. At 211°, one has really hot water; at 212°, one has steam. The poster illustrates that steam can power a locomotive! The poster points out how that one additional degree changes everything and makes all the difference.

There is a certain amount of fissile material needed to maintain a nuclear chain reaction; this is referred to as critical mass. Principals can think of school capacity building and cultural transformation in the terms of critical mass. There is a certain amount of effort by a certain number of educators that will transform a school's culture; that is a fact. From one thing, another will be formed; yet the trickiest part is knowing what constitutes critical mass, or what is the "one additional degree" for your school.

Unlike the laws of physics, there exists no prescribed formula for reaching a cultural critical mass. Heck and Hallinger (2009) suggest that school leadership and capacity building "are mutually reinforcing in their effects on each other over time. This reciprocal effects model of school improvement is underpinned by the notion that in settings where people perceive stronger distributed leadership, schools appear better able to improve their academic improvement capacity" (p. 35).

Cultural critical mass will be unique to each school because we are dealing with collective human behavior, which defies pigeonholing. Have you ever asked yourself why two schools in the same district that enroll students from the same demographic pool and employ teachers who possess similar training and qualifications arrive at vastly different student outcomes?

While no one can accurately predict which person, initiative, or idea will be the one to tip the scales and create a synergistic culture that is larger than the sum of its parts, there is much recorded in teacher leadership literature about the many paths which lead to one goal: a school culture where teacher leadership is the norm.

Danielson (2007) puts forth four prevailing conditions that promote teacher leadership. "Not every school is hospitable to the emergence of teacher leaders, particularly informal teacher leaders. The school administrator plays a crucial role in fostering the conditions that facilitate teacher leadership" (p. 18). Danielson describes these conditions as:

- A safe environment for risk taking
- Opportunities to learn leadership skills
- Administrators who encourage teacher-leaders
- Absence of the "tall poppy syndrome"

Danielson uses the term "tall poppy syndrome" to refer to the problem of colleagues not wanting their peers to become teacher-leaders, meaning that those "who stick their heads up risk being cut down to size" (p. 19) by their fellow teachers.

Harris (2003) found three prevailing conditions which principals must have in place for teacher leadership to occur:

- Teachers need time set aside to plan and participate in developing school-wide plans, leading study groups, organizing visits to other schools, collaborating with Higher Education Institutions (HEIs), and collaborating with colleagues (pp. 219–220).
- Opportunities for continuous professional development must be rich and diverse. Teacher leadership needs to focus on aspects specific to their leadership roles, and not just on the development of teaching skills and knowledge (p. 220).
- Teachers' self-confidence to act as leaders in their schools is essential to capacity building. Teacher leadership happens when teachers are fully developed in their leadership potential through networking and structured programs, which results in transformation of the school (p. 220).

While the prevailing conditions identified by Danielson and Harris relate to principals support of teacher-leaders, Harrison and Killion (2007) identified ten roles in which teacher-leaders can help their colleagues:

1. *Resource Provider*—shares instructional resources with colleagues
2. *Instructional Specialist*—implements effective teaching strategies
3. *Curriculum Specialist*—helps with how various components of the curriculum and the content standards link together
4. *Classroom Supporter*—works inside classrooms to coteach, demonstrate lessons, observe, and provide feedback
5. *Learning Facilitator*—creates opportunities to have teachers learn from each other
6. *Mentor*—mentoring novice teachers and acclimating new teachers to the school
7. *School Leader*—holds traditionally formalized leadership roles such as department chair or serving on any of the various committees
8. *Data Coach*—assists teachers to wade through data and turn it into useful information
9. *Catalyst for Change*—pushes the school out of the status quo and toward a vision
10. *Learner (one of the most important leadership roles)*—role model who seeks continual improvement and explores new strategies

Much of the success or failure of teacher leadership depends upon relationships, and healthy relationships are dependent upon trust. Donaldson (2007) put it succinctly; whether it is principals, teacher-leaders, or both, "the leadership litmus test is, are the relationships in this school mobilizing people to improve learning for all students?" (p. 29).

In Summary

Principals wishing to transform the culture of their schools, whether new or veteran, don't know what they don't know. Gaining situational awareness is key. Situational awareness is gained through the principal being out of his or her office and in the building. Another way is through polling stakeholders.

The principal's initial step is to conduct a needs assessment, which may include all stakeholders, but must include the teachers. Next, the principal shares the results of the needs assessment with the teachers. Through this process, the principal and the teachers build a common understanding of the needs of the school and a shared vision of what needs to be accomplished.

To build momentum, the principal concentrates on the "small wins" first. Small wins are the most powerful lever to overcome resistance and promote buy-in on the road to improving morale and effective practice (Schmoker, 2006b). It is wise to begin by concentrating on teacher priorities *before* focusing on principal priorities.

Use this momentum to enlist the help of teachers and engage them in safe risk taking. Successful risk taking will not only help to build trust, but also encourage more teachers' risk taking. Successful experiences trusting the principal, other teacher-leaders, and teachers will build healthy relationships.

It is important to work to abolish the myth of the heroic leader, and move away from transactional leadership that fosters an "us and them" culture. A more transformational leadership of collaboration will foster the notion of distributive leadership. The principal cannot simply assign leader roles in an ineffectual "leader-plus" model, but must truly foster teacher leadership, where the teacher-leaders have a legitimate role in the school's decision-making process.

Shaping a school culture takes time and cannot be done alone. A new kind of relationship between teachers and the principal will emerge with enough trust and small wins momentum. While the difference between hot water and steam is only one degree, the principal cannot forget that he or she must apply the first 211° of heat before reaching 212°; it may take between 3 and 5 years to make sustainable changes to the culture of a school.

Chapter Discussion Questions

1. Stepping out of one's comfort zone can be scary. Please write down an appropriate risk, a baby step, that you could take in the next week that involves fostering teacher leadership.
2. If intellectual stimulation comes from allowing subordinates to question traditional beliefs, then (Yukl, 1999):
   a. Can subordinates in your school question traditions?
   b. Are the faculty and staff free to look at problems in a different way?
   c. Is your school's culture receptive to innovative solutions to problems? If so, how? If not, how could it be made more receptive?
3. Provide some examples of the difference between the "what" and the "how" of leadership.
4. Make a list of what Principal Roberta did well when she took over at the Sorrin School. What would you have done differently and why?

8   School Climate and Culture

In some South Pacific cultures, a speaker holds a conch shell as a symbol of temporary position of authority. Leaders must understand who holds the conch; that is, who should be listened to and when.

—MAX DE PREE

DEFINING SCHOOL CLIMATE AND CULTURE

This chapter is about time and change. While school "climate" and "culture" are similar, in that each term describes a condition brought about by the state of interpersonal relationships in schools that impacts the social and professional atmosphere, one is fleeting while the other is enduring. There exists no universal understanding of the terms "climate" and "culture" as they relate to schools (Cohen, McCabe, Michelli, & Pickeral, 2009), which may explain why so many people associated with schools seem to use the terms "climate" and "culture" interchangeably; or even more confusingly, someone might refer to "climate" when speaking of what another means when he or she speaks of "culture," and vice versa.

These terms for the purposes of this text are not synonymous with each other, and they possess distinct meanings. The interchangeability of the terms "climate" and "culture" can make the study of these topics confusing. A number of researchers define climate to mean what other researchers define as culture. An example is that Van Houtte (2005) and Stronge and Leeper (2012) see climate as enduring, while Schen and Teddlie (2008) view culture not as a subset of climate but the other way around, asserting "that climate is better understood as a level of school culture" (p. 130).

Schen and Teddlie clarified their position on the subject. "Van Houtte subsumes culture under climate but nonetheless concludes that it is culture that holds the most promise for future research on school improvement" (p. 129). Schen and Teddlie "arrived at a somewhat different conceptualization of school culture than that described by Van Houtte" and "propose that school climate may more appropriately be thought of as a subset of the broader construct of school culture" (p. 129).

Absent an absolute definition, we concur with Schen and Teddlie. In this text, we have elected to refer to "climate" as meaning that which is less enduring, while defining "culture" as that which is more enduring. We have not substituted terminology in any of the original researcher's direct quotes; the reader will quickly recognize that the researchers quoted throughout this chapter do not use "climate" and "culture" consistently; yet, it should be easy for the reader to distinguish those researchers who refer to enduring interpersonal relationships as "culture" from those who refer to them as "climate." We are hopeful the inconsistent terminology will not detract from the reader's enjoyment or ability to explore ideas presented within this chapter.

SCHOOL CLIMATE

The term "school climate" is sociological in nature. Climate describes the more transient qualities of collective school relationships, such as describing the energy of the staff on any given day. School climate is the influence of collective behavior or, more accurately, collective perceptions. Unlike meteorological climate, school climate is subject to daily, even hourly, changes. It is less enduring than school culture. School climate is more like the weather: variable and constantly changing.

If the school community were to learn of the death of a beloved student or teacher, the climate would change instantly. A somber tenor would pervade the school building and alter the collective mood or outlook of the school community. This is not to say that the culture is unaffected by significant changes in climate; quite the contrary is true.

SCHOOL CULTURE

Typically, the culture of a school will not change rapidly. Culture is the culmination of school climate over weeks, months, and years. Culture is like looking at a trend instead of one piece of data. A school's culture is impacted by how those in the school community respond to all the big and small climate changes over time.

The culture of a school evolves over time. The traditions, expectations, mores, norms, and established routines are part and parcel of the school's culture. How the school responds to the loss of a beloved member of the school community is influenced by the school's culture. Some school cultures would expect to close school for a memorial ceremony, while other school cultures would carry on with business as usual out of respect for the deceased and a sense of duty. One path is not an absolute wrong while the other is an absolute right; these are culturally dependent decisions.

Cohen, McCabe, Michelli, and Pickeral (2009) define school culture (for which they instead use the term school climate) as "the quality and character of school life. School climate is based on patterns of people's experiences of school life and reflects norms, goals, values, interpersonal relationships, teaching and learning practices, and organizational structures" (p. 182).

Cohen et al. identified the four essential dimensions of school culture as:

1. *Safety*—both physical and social/emotional
2. *Teaching and Learning*—including quality of instruction; social, emotional, and ethical learning; professional development; and leadership
3. *Relationships*—including respect for diversity; school community and collaboration; and morale and connectedness
4. *Environmental/Structure*—including cleanliness; adequate space; materials; and so on

Cohen, McCabe, Michelli, and Pickeral (2009) suggest that a sustainable, positive school culture has implications beyond the school and "fosters youth development and learning necessary for a productive, contributive, and satisfying life in a democratic society" (p. 182). This vision of a school culture includes "norms, values, and expectations that support people feeling socially, emotionally, and physically safe. People are engaged and respected" (p. 182).

While recognizing the importance of assessing student academic performance, Cohen, Fege, and Pickeral (2009) warn that "solely reporting on test scores does not provide the public sufficient information about the quality of teaching and learning in the school or the school district" (p. 2). Cohen et al. suggest instead that schools should provide a comprehensive picture of student and school performance that moves beyond academic assessments to include the "social, emotional, and developmental needs of the student" (p 2). Cohen et al. view school culture and environment "at the apex of this evaluative process" (p. 2).

THE ROLE OF THE PRINCIPAL IN CHANGING SCHOOL CULTURE

It takes the school leader one instant to influence climate, but years to change culture. One of the biggest rookie mistakes for school principals taking up the principalship in a new school is to try to institute cultural change too quickly.

Changing school culture is a lot like boiling a frog. Boiling a frog slowly is an age-old metaphor, and it was even brought to life in a scientific experiment (Scripture, 1897). As the story goes, a frog thrown into a boiling pot will immediately hop out, but if the frog is placed in a pot and the temperature of the water is brought to a boil gradually enough, the frog will remain unaware and not hop out of the pot. While some climatic changes in schools need to be conducted with swift decisiveness, changing the culture of a school is more like boiling a frog. One of Principal Roberta's college professors used to say, "People don't mind change, it is being changed that people are opposed to." Stated another way, people want to be a part of the change, not have it *done to* them.

This notion of principals building a school culture with a shared common vision is nothing new. Perry (1908) spoke of it over a hundred years ago. He called school culture by a different name, *esprit de corps*, but his message was still clear. Perry also spoke of what in modern day parlance we might describe as *synergy*. "The morale of the school should be something more than what is brought out by the sum of the independent efforts of all the teachers" (p. 332).

Today, the principal's ability to foster a positive culture has found its way into principal evaluation models. An example of this is in the Commonwealth of Virginia, where the new principal evaluation system (Stronge & Leeper, 2012) includes evaluating principals on school culture (which they instead term climate) as one of the performance standards.

To answer the question "What does school culture mean?," Stronge and Leeper said that school culture "is the relatively enduring quality of the school environment that is experienced by participants, affects their behavior, and is based on their collective perception about behavior in schools" (Stronge & Leeper, 2012, p. 6). Stronge and Leeper describe school culture as referring to the social and working relationships of staff and principals. They speak of the feeling you get when you enter the school's front office, or as you walk down the halls. They describe climate as the behaviors noticed and the energy level of teachers and students in classrooms. Another factor is how well the school community works as a team. For Stronge and Leeper, these are crucial factors that affect school culture.

HOW PRINCIPALS INFLUENCE CLIMATE AND CULTURE

Principals and teacher-leaders both impact climate and culture. How these leadership positions work together can be likened to dance partners. New principals need to understand first and foremost that, in the beginning, *they* are the change. It is important for both teacher-leaders and principals to recognize that, in the beginning, they may unintentionally step on the other's toes.

Having someone new sitting in the big chair is a huge adjustment for a school community. A hundred concerns are running through the minds of the faculty and staff when someone new takes the reins. They want to know if the new principal will think they are doing a good job or not because they want to know if they will be asked to change. Even the worst-performing schools have pieces of their cultural identity that they value and do not want to see go away.

There are all sorts of entry plans for school administrators; many suggest an entry plan for the first 90 or 100 days in the new school, others for the first year. Transitioning in as principal at a new school is an important time. Transitioning as the leader of a new school is not about instituting a series of objectives to be checked off according to dates on the calendar. Transitioning in to lead a new school is all about acclimating to the school's culture. It is critical to learn what is cherished about the existing culture and why.

There was a new principal who took over the principalship in July, before the teachers returned. She thought that she would create a physical representation that she was a leader of action. She wanted to distinguish her leadership from that of her predecessor. So this principal decided to spruce up the place, with the idea of having the faculty return to a physically appealing school both inside and out. One of her ideas was to have the shrubs outside the school removed and replaced with flowers. The custodian attempted to protest, but she was having none of it; she was on a mission.

When the teachers returned to school, they were horrified to find that the shrubs planted in commemoration of the passing of a much-loved and long-tenured teacher had been ripped out. These shrubs, representing the school community's memorial to a beloved colleague and teacher, had been irrevocably destroyed. An unfavorable first impression was indelibly etched in the minds of the faculty, staff, parents, and student community before this principal even met them. This principal, with such high hopes of making a lasting impact as a principal, never recovered from this one seemingly insignificant decision.

New principals can reach out to faculty from the beginning to better understand the culture and identity the formal and informal teacher-leaders among them. The principal who shows a willingness to first understand before making a point of being understood will start off on the right foot. It is not just new principals who may be developing teacher-leaders. The veteran principal will have the advantage of knowing who among the staff are teacher-leaders, but may also have to overcome the hurdle of reinventing an organization with an existing and well-established hierarchical structure. In many ways, the fresh start may give the newly appointed principal an advantage in influencing a culture receptive to teacher leadership.

BUILDING UNITY

The principal is the visionary who can lead the school in the development of a shared vision. Teachers are more likely to invest their time and energy in becoming teacher-leaders if they feel their efforts will advance a mission to which they and their colleagues are committed.

Building unity around a common goal is the foundation upon which a school culture is constructed. Culture boils down to a shared passion for something, whether that something is antique automobiles, a favorite rock band, a political party, or a group of people dedicated to improving the lives of children. The quote attributed to Margaret Mead rings true for those committed to mindful school cultures: "Never doubt that a small group of thoughtful, committed citizens can change the world. Indeed, it is the only thing that ever has."

Building unity can be accomplished through celebrating success. Barkley, Bottoms, Feagin, and Clark (2001) emphasize that maintaining motivation and effort requires building unity around group goals. "A winning team celebrates after the game and returns to practice the next day to continue developing skills" (p. 31). Celebrations in schools can take on many forms. Principal Roberta celebrated wins in the school newsletter, with complimentary notes to teachers often cc'd to their personnel file, and with an end-of-year faculty meeting dedicated to a shout-out recognizing faculty contributions.

Michael F. was a first-time elementary school principal in a bucolic rural community nestled in the foothills. Michael instituted a community celebration held on Friday afternoons in the gymnasium. The school community was invited to witness the accomplishments of students and, by extension, their teachers. These accomplishments were not limited to academics; accomplishments in art, music, and physical education were also celebrated. It was an event that reinforced the shared cultural beliefs of that school.

One Friday, some unforeseen event caused this celebration to run late. The teachers were certain with the school buses pulling up outside the school that Michael would pull the plug and reschedule a time to recognize the last two students in that Friday's celebration. Michael explained that the school buses would just have to wait. The school community had gathered to recognize all the students being honored, and these young performers would be no exception.

If actions speak louder than words, Michael's actions "spoke" a strong message to the teachers, students, parents, and grandparents gathered in the audience that afternoon. The unspoken message was that the leader of the school valued the cultural importance of celebrating successes and recognizing accomplishments.

A CULTURE OF DISTRIBUTIVE LEADERSHIP

Distributive leadership, when first implemented, can feel like turning left when you want to go right. Even some long-time motorcyclists are surprised to learn about countersteering. Countersteering is utterly counterintuitive. It is a technique for initiating a turn when operating a motorcycle, or even a bicycle. This technique requires momentarily turning the handlebars in the *opposite* direction from the way the cyclist intends for the bike to turn. This adjustment causes the bike and its rider to lean, and thus improves the bike's ability to negotiate the curve and make a tighter turn (Fajans, 2000).

Similar to the uncertainty experienced the first time the operator of a motorcycle decides to countersteer by turning the handlebars of a moving motorcycle in the "wrong" direction just as it is heading into a turn, it may seem sickeningly counterintuitive to work and study for years to become the leader of a school only to then allow others to help steer the school. Both the motorcyclist and the principal are worried about the outcome of heading in an unintended direction.

Harris (2003) recognized that the first step in distributed leadership "requires those in formal leadership positions to relinquish power to others. Apart from the challenge to authority and ego, this potentially places the head or principal in a vulnerable position because of the lack of direct control over certain activities" (p. 319). Many principals lead through their authority, making that first difficult step of relinquishing sole control of the school a significant paradigm shift. Principals who have only experienced working in a hierarchical structure and have not experienced a culture of shared leadership may find "countersteering" their school in a new direction rife with anxiety. However difficult taking that first step may be, it is necessary if a principal hopes to establish a true distributive leadership structure. Harris also found that the "top-down" approach to leadership is mutually exclusive to distributive leadership, and that "the internal school structures offer significant impediments to the development of distributed leadership. The current hierarchy of leadership within both primary and secondary schools means that power resides with the leadership team, i.e., at the top of the school" (p. 319).

Harris claims that the most important aspect of distributed leadership is how leadership is distributed and by whom. Assigning teachers extra jobs does not represent distributive leadership. "If it [leadership distribution] remains the case that the head distributes leadership responsibilities to teachers, then distributed leadership becomes nothing more than informed delegation" (p. 319).

A CULTURE OF TRUST

The principal models trust by making himself or herself vulnerable. Tschannen-Moran (2011) defines trust as "one party's willingness to be vulnerable to another party based upon the confidence that the latter party is benevolent, honest, open, reliable, and competent" (p. 3). This willingness to make oneself vulnerable is an essential piece of shifting a culture. The principal, as formal leader, is the one who demonstrates to all the potential informal leaders a willingness to take a risk.

Tschannen-Moran found that it was trust in the principal, and not transformational leadership behaviors, that most inspired followers to greater citizenship. "Trust in the principal was found to be a predictor of organizational citizenship behaviors"

(Tschannen-Moran, 2011, p. 7). Conversely, breaking the trust with teachers and teacher-leaders can have long-lasting negative effects on a principal's ability to change school culture in a positive direction. "When trust is broken between administrators and teachers, suspicion and psychological withdrawal are likely to result" (p. 12).

A CULTURE OF COLLECTIVE MINDFULNESS

D. S. Black (2010) offers a four-part definition of mindfulness (p. 1):

1. An open and receptive attention to and awareness of what is occurring in the present moment
2. An awareness that arises through intentionally attending in an open, accepting, and discerning way to whatever is arising in the present moment
3. An attention that is receptive to the whole field of awareness and remains in an open state so that it can be directed to currently experienced sensations, thoughts, emotions, and memories
4. Stated simply, waking up from a life on automatic pilot

Black contrasts the mindfulness of being fully present with mindlessness of not being fully present. It's through a focusing on intentionality that leaders discover the many unintentional outcomes as a result of not being mindful.

Smith and Scarbrough (2011) posit that mindfulness and trust have to go hand in hand when principals build a culture of trust. They discovered that "principals who exhibit honesty, openness, reliability, competence, and benevolence develop high levels of trust with teachers. This, in turn, encourages the openness and intimacy necessary to cultivate mindful and focused actions among salient stakeholder groups" (pp. 38–39). Each one of the traits identified by Smith and Scarbrough—honesty, openness, reliability, competence, and benevolence—carry with them a lot of power to persuade or dissuade potential followers.

Smith and Scarbrough (2011) suggest that teachers associate trust with mindfulness. "Trust in the principal emerged as a very strong predictor of principal mindfulness. In brief, teachers who exhibit high levels of trust in their principal are more apt to perceive their principal as being more mindful in leading the school" (p. 33). The goal of the principal is to create a culture of collective mindfulness.

A culture of collective mindfulness calls for a change from what, in many cases, is the prevailing view of concentrating on "what is wrong with schools today." Hoy and Tarter (2011) call for educational research to shift from its critical "what is wrong with schools" focus and play a much more important and positive role in improving schools by beginning to study what is *good* about schools. "Our goal should be to find actions that lead to healthy, engaging, meaningful, and thriving schools where students flourish, learn, and are happy" (p. 429). Hoy and Tarter suggest that organizational trust is a key component to creating the kind of improved schoolwork systems that support the greatest satisfaction among administrators and teachers. When the contemporary trend of focusing on the negative rather than the positive is reversed, teachers' lives will become more fulfilling, and as a result so too will student's lives.

Mwangi (2011) credits the creation of a culture of collective mindfulness to altering school culture. Mwangi suggests that it is through the powerful qualities of "receptive awareness, alertness, and reflection that collective mindfulness inculcates schools that are collectively mindful, [and] have a powerful means of monitoring their policies and practices. Such a mindfulness culture would assist schools to abandon obsolete practices subtly embedded in the school context" (p. 34).

HELPING THE TEACHER-LEADERS TO HELP THEMSELVES

Leithwood, Harris, and Hopkins (2008) found that heroic lone-leader aspirations actually "do more to discourage potential candidates from applying for leadership jobs than they do to improve the quality of incumbent leadership" (p. 32). Peter Drucker, renowned for his many contributions to business thinking, believed that no institution can survive if it needs geniuses or supermen to manage it. It must be organized to get along under a leadership of average human beings.

Leithwood et al. contended that "[s]chool leaders improve teaching and learning indirectly and most powerfully through their influence on staff motivation, commitment, and working conditions" (p. 32). Entrusting leadership to only a few does not significantly improve working conditions, and leaves those "nonleaders" to feel that the school structure is still "top-down," only with more bosses on top. Ash and Persall (2000) argue that "creating an organizational culture and infrastructure that supports leadership opportunities for everyone—a "leader-full" organization—requires principals to have an altogether different set of leadership skills than have previously been necessary" (p. 15). Leithwood et al. (2008) propose that "school leadership has a greater influence on schools and pupils when it is widely distributed" (p. 34).

Grant (2008) described three types of distributive leadership: authorized, dispersed, and democratic. Authorized distributed leadership is "where tasks are distributed from the principal to others in a hierarchical system of relations where the principal has positional authority" (p. 87). Dispersed distributed leadership refers to an emergent, more autonomous process in which "much of the workings of an organization take place without the formal working of a hierarchy" (p. 87). Related to dispersed distributed leadership, democratic distributed leadership shares the emergent and concertive nature, yet democratic distributed leadership critically engages organizational values and goals and does not assume political neutrality. Leithwood et al. (2008) suggest that not all patterns of distribution are equally effective and attempt to address the questions, "Why are some leaders more expert than others?" and "Why do some people seem to develop leadership capacities to higher levels and more quickly than others?" (p. 36). Leithwood et al found evidence to support the claim that under challenging circumstances "most successful school leaders are open-minded and ready to learn from others" (p. 36). Principals who are "flexible rather than dogmatic in their thinking within a system of core values, persistent (e.g., in pursuit of high expectations of staff motivation, commitment, learning, and achievement for all), resilient, and optimistic"(p. 36) can more successfully face "daunting conditions [and] are often able to push forward when there is little reason to expect progress" (p. 36).

REFRAMING THE PERCEPTIONS OF LEADERSHIP

If the principal does not actively embrace a model of distributive leadership, then a cultural change is unlikely to take root in the school. The principal needs to actively promote a new vision of what leadership looks like within the school culture, and clearly articulate to teacher-leaders how teacher leadership is going to be evaluated within the school. Lambert (2002) suggests that school leadership is about learning together and must be "a broad concept that is distinguished from person, role, and a discrete set of individual behaviours. It needs to be embedded in the school community as a whole, which suggests a shared responsibility for a shared purpose of community" (p. 1). Lambert spoke to the folly of equating "leadership" with "leader." She refers to this as "trait theory," which causes principals and potential teacher-leaders to think, "if only a leader had these certain traits, we would have good leadership. This tendency causes those who might otherwise roll up their sleeves, pitch in and help, to abstain from the work of leadership—abdicating both responsibilities and opportunities" (p. 1).

Harris (2008), in speaking about distributive leadership, urged readers to move "beyond trying to understand leadership through the actions and beliefs of single leaders" and to a place of "understanding leadership as a dynamic organisational entity" (pp. 173–174). Harris did not view leadership capacity or capability in schools as fixed. Harris calls on those in formal leadership roles to support those in informal leadership roles. Carrying out this support requires understanding of need for a responsive flexible, fluid, and creative leadership structure. If cultural sustainability is to be achieved in schools, the formal leaders have to realize that "as different people seek and are tacitly or openly granted leadership functions, a dynamic pattern of distributed leadership gradually takes over" (p. 174). Harris is quick to point out that this "distributed leadership does not imply that the formal leadership structures within organisations are removed or redundant. Instead, it is assumed that there is a powerful relationship between vertical and lateral leadership processes" (p. 174).

SEPARATING THE PRACTICE FROM THE PRACTITIONER

The principal must strengthen the teacher-leader's ability to constructively deal with interpersonal conflict. It is essential in professional dialog for the teacher-leaders to be able to separate the practice from the practitioner. One of the forums where teacher-leaders will influence school practice is in professional learning communities or communities of practice. It is important to develop clear protocols for professional learning communities that focus on assessing what is learned instead of focusing on what is taught.

The findings of Wahlstrom and Louis (2008) suggest that when "teachers are involved in making decisions that affect them, they tend to strengthen or deepen their instructional practice" (p. 483). Yet Wahlstrom and Louis warn that strong professional learning communities, which come together for the purposes of sharing practices rather than for decision making, may, as teacher dependence on the principal wanes, actually create an environment that is less trustful of the principal. "This lessened dependence may help to account for the diminished impact of trust in leadership when we take the level of professional community into account" (p. 483).

Principal Roberta invited a professor from the nearby state university's education department to a faculty meeting to clarify the distinctions between a team meeting or common planning time with that of a community of practice. When communities of practice meet at the Sorrin School, the teachers have a laser-like focus on what is learned instead of the typical approach of what is taught. The teachers have found that focusing on what is taught is ineffectual; just because something is *taught* does not mean it is learned; improved instruction comes from analyzing what is *learned*. Superior instruction comes from analyzing the quality and extent to which what has been retained has been applied in different settings (higher order thinking skills). Through the use of a meeting protocol, student work is at the heart of CoPs (communities of practice). Through a cycle of inquiry, student work is analyzed. Teachers then backward design their practice to bring about changes in instructional practices to make improvement in student learning. Student work can be anything from formal assessments to simply random work samples. The results of CoP analysis are then used to make positive adaptations in curriculum, instruction, and assessment.

Sorrin communities of practice are never about a practitioner. This concept was the most difficult for teachers to wrap their heads around, but when they did it was found that teachers could engage in what would otherwise be difficult conversations with colleagues. The Sorrin staff is well on the road to seeing themselves as fellow learners on a journey. The notion of "good" teachers or "bad" teachers has been replaced because of the finality of the either/or scenario. Principal Roberta reports the necessity of reshaping the culture of either "good" or "bad" teachers because it presumed that only the "bad" ones needed improvement while the "good" ones, having arrived at "good" status, did not need to improve. Instead, the Sorrin School supports a view of a learning spectrum where teachers, administrators, and students fall somewhere along the learning spectrum. This view holds that nobody ever "arrives" at a destination, but instead everyone continues to move further along this spectrum regardless of learning stage. When viewed as fellow journeyers at different stages along the same spectrum, the Sorrin faculty is able to focus on improving practice instead of finding flaws with the practitioner.

Roberta recognizes making the distinction between practice and practitioner as key to holding the difficult conversations necessary for educators to challenge one another. Teachers spend each day correcting children, but when asked to openly—albeit constructively—offer criticism to teaching colleagues, most will demur. As educators, we shy away from criticizing colleagues; we find it uncomfortable, because what if those colleagues were to turn around and criticize us? We are not conditioned to openly ask others to shine a spotlight on the weaknesses in our practice, yet outside critique is the model we use to move students forward on their educational journey along the learning spectrum. Teachers do not belittle students by having them reflect upon their work.

Roberta began the process of pedagogical cross-pollination by asking the most comfortable teachers to open their classrooms to their colleagues. She enlisted a retired professor of education from the local college to begin voluntary instructional rounds with small groups of teachers observing each other's instruction. Initially observers have a very narrow scope, which is identified by the teacher volunteering to be observed as an area of concern. Roberta emphasizes that instructional rounds are about improving practice and professional growth, not for evaluation, in any way high stakes, or practitioner-centric.

In Summary

School climate and culture are as distinct from each other, yet as interconnected, as metrological weather and climate. Climate is the state of collective interpersonal relationships in the moment, while culture is the result of the culmination of those moments over time. It is essential that principals do not attempt to rush the process of changing the culture of a school. This does not imply that principals should not work consistently to change the school culture, only that it can take several years to influence sustainable change.

The principal next turns his or her focus on developing a shared vision to build unity. Building unity can be accomplished through celebrating each success along the path toward reaching that vision. It should be noted that a common vision is a dynamic goal, one that is revisited so it can change and evolve over time to meet the ever-changing needs of the school.

The principal is a player, but not the only player in building trusting relationships among the staff. An effort should be made by the staff and the principal to make a distinction between the practice and the practitioner. Recognizing this distinction allows difficult conversations to be not only tolerated but expected. Building trusting relationships begins with the principal's willingness to be vulnerable and step out of the traditional "top-down" leadership structure. Trusting the staff is the first step toward modeling reciprocal trust.

Hand-in-hand with reciprocal trust is collective mindfulness, an intentionality of what we do, why we do it, and how it impacts our school culture. The principal and teachers must strive to possess the receptive awareness, alertness, and reflection, which Mwangi (2011) described as essential to abandoning the obsolete practices of the past.

With unity behind a common vision, reciprocal trust, and collective mindfulness in place, the formal leader relinquishes control and the informal leaders can take on increasingly more vital leadership roles. As Harris (2008) emphasized, distributing leadership to teacher-leaders does not lessen the principal's role. This new leadership paradigm reframes the previous connotation of the principal.

In this new paradigm, the principal helps the teachers help themselves. This shift in principal focus toward supporting the teacher-leaders in an ever-changing educational environment supports teacher collaboration and fosters the development of teacher leadership. The emergence of teacher leadership will inevitably support a common vision that is reflected in the curriculum, instruction, assessment, and environmental factors influencing the broader school culture. This will create a virtuous cycle/circle, or the opposite of a vicious cycle. The more leader-full the school becomes, the more invested the faculty becomes; the more invested the faculty becomes, the more the culture improves; the more the culture improves, the more conducive it is to individuals taking the risk of becoming teacher-leaders. Let us not lose sight of the original rationale for embarking upon change, that the ultimate beneficiaries of leader-full schools are the students whose opportunities to achieve are greatly improved.

The benefits of helping teachers help students are not new. Over 100 years ago, Perry (1908) spoke of how the "underlying duty of the principal" was to help teachers serve their pupils. He went on to declare that in proportion to how much the principal helped the teachers, the principal, in return, would be rewarded with a loyal staff and the recognition of leading a school that helps students. Teacher leadership is the natural next step in the complexity of leading modern schools. For over 100 years, it has been recognized that fostering a culture that supports teachers helps not only teachers and students, but principals as well, which makes it surprising that more leader-full school cultures do not exist.

Chapter Discussion Questions

1. Answer the following cultural entry plan questions for new principals.
   a. What parts of the school culture does this community value?
   b. Who are the teacher-leaders in your school?
   c. Have the teacher-leaders been encouraged to share leadership, been stifled, or has the topic simply been ignored?
   d. What is your school community's self-perception?
2. List four examples of "informed delegation" and four examples of distributed leadership. How do your examples of informed delegation and distributed leadership differ?
3. If you were to be more mindful in your role at school, how would others know?
4. Lambert cautions of the folly of "trait theory" or equating "leadership" with "leader." Identify three ways in which this thinking can be reversed in your school.
5. Identify three practices where you struggle to separate yourself from your practice.

CHAPTER

9

Building Sustainability

You can never have an impact on society if you have not changed yourself.

—NELSON MANDELA

This chapter is about building the sustainability of innovative efforts and school culture. Most principals would accept that "research supports the correlation between a positive school climate [culture] and improved student achievement" (Black, 2010, p. 460). Deal and Peterson (1999) go further to describe school culture as permeating everything: "the way people act, how they dress, what they talk about or avoid talking about, whether they seek out colleagues for help or don't, and how teachers feel about their work and their students" (p. 3). The goal for principals is to bring about a sustainable reculturation that results in sustainable student achievement.

In farming, sustainability is a term used to describe a method of harvesting that does not permanently deplete or damage a resource, so that it can be utilized again and again. For school leaders sustainability holds a similar meaning. If a school culture is to be sustainable, the gains achieved by all of the hard work and effort put into building a school culture supportive of teacher leadership should be seen as a renewable resource. The research of Lipson, Mosenthal, Mekkelsen and Russ (2004) points out with abundant clarity that "successful schools do not happen by accident, and they are not guaranteed by the presence of nice families and orderly classrooms. Rather, success is fashioned by the educators, students and community members in a way that is context-specific" (p. 534).

It takes a concerted, organized effort to positively change a school and its culture. "Schools put themselves in the driver's seat when they invest in professional development and collaborative cultures that focus on student learning and associated improvements in instructional practices" (Fullan, 1998, p. 9). Fostering teacher leadership is not a onetime, short-term initiative. Sustained teacher leadership requires a culture that supports it. Unsustainable achievements, no matter how temporarily impactful, will simply be swept away by the next principal. Peters (2011) found that principals often enter a new school with little or no overlap to their predecessors and begin their new jobs with an expectation "to lead the school in a new and different direction" (p. 68).

Principals will make better decisions if they are cognizant of the distinct difference between restructuring and reculturing. Fullan (1997) contends that restructuring is about things. "Restructuring refers to changes in the formal structure of schooling in terms of organization, timetables, roles, and the like. Restructuring bears no direct relationship to improvements in teaching and learning" (p. 10). Reculturing is about people. "Reculturing, by contrast, involves changing the norms, values, incentives, skills, and relationships in the organization to foster a different way of working together. Reculturing makes a difference in teaching and learning" (p. 10).

The Boston Teacher Leadership Resource Center (2012) has identified a list of conditions necessary to foster informal teacher leadership:

1. *Strategic teaming*—providing teachers time to share teaching and learning ideas
2. *Data routines*—regular review of evidence to inform teaching and learning
3. *Culture of shared ownership*—a culture where frank feedback between colleagues about instruction is expected to be given and received
4. *Inventory of professional expertise*—knowing who are the go-to experts among us
5. *Communication structures*—a system for quick answers to teacher and learning inquiries
6. *Access to professional knowledge base*—disseminating research resources so that best practices are practiced
7. *Involvement of family and community*—including families and communities in school conversations

When a school is recultured to foster teacher leadership, each of these conditions would be evident.

ETHICAL LEADERSHIP FOR THE COMMON GOOD

School leaders do not lead *things*; they lead *people*. The people led—teachers—have an enormous impact on other people—students. School principals must consider the ethical implications for those impacted by their decisions. Ethical and moral are often used interchangeably. Starratt (2012) points out that some scholars make the distinction between ethical behavior and moral behavior by indicating that the former has an internal set of guiding principles, while the latter's behaviors are externally influenced.

Whether the school principal uses the terms moral and ethical interchangeably or not, there exists an obligation, moral or ethical or both, to carry out interactions with other human beings with integrity. School principals, as the leader of leaders, sometimes shy away from the topic of the ethical treatment of emergent teacher-leaders. This is not about a principal becoming a preacher and decreeing absolute right and wrongs; it is about not excluding ethics on the path toward becoming a more reflective school leader. "The cultivation of an ethical school does not involve superimposing a set of demands on an already overburdened educating work. Rather it involves educators practicing their profession with an integrity that goes right to the core of their work" (Starratt, 2012, p. 3).

Starratt (2004a) calls for school leaders to reconsider what actions are associated with the ethical leadership of people. Ethical school leaders understand that leadership decisions carry with them a reverberating impact on the lives of human beings. Ethical leadership requires school principals to fully embrace the human condition when making decisions. "As a human being, the leader is responsible for taking a stand with other human beings—not above them, as someone removed from the human condition, but as one sharing fully in it" (p. 49).

Starratt (2004b) identified five domains, or roles, of the ethical responsibility of school leaders as: a human being, a citizen and public servant, an educator, an educational administrator, and an educational leader. Each role is inseparable from the ones that go before it; the school leader can never divest her or himself from also being an administrator, educator, public servant, or human being. This necessitates that those principals act with ethical responsibility and treat "everyone in the school as human beings with care and compassion, treating them as citizens with rights and responsibilities in the pursuit of the common good. . ." (p. 131).

SYSTEMIC APPROACH

It is worth pointing out that *systemic* and *systematic* are not interchangeable terms. *Systemic* is defined as "system-wide or deeply engrained in the system. It usually applies to habits or processes that are difficult to reverse because they are built into a system." *Systematic* refers to carrying "out step-by-step procedures" (Grammarist, 2012). We are referring to establishing habits or processes that will be difficult to reverse because they will be built into the system, not step-by-step procedures.

Systemic usually applies to carefully planned processes that unfold gradually. Adopting a systemic approach to reculturing schools around teacher leadership will benefit both principals and teacher-leaders. Fullan (1999) refers to organizations as *living systems* and understanding them as such is key to their longevity. "This gives deeper meaning to the phrase that people and relationships are critical. It is the quality of the relationships among organizational members, as they evolve, that makes for long-term success" (p. 13). Long-term success requires a long-term, big-picture perspective. A school culture cannot achieve long-term sustainability if its successes rest upon the shoulders of one or two charismatic or visionary superleaders. Those who comprise the school community must be individually, as well as collectively, invested in fostering *their* common culture. It is essential that schools possess effective systems that support and reflect the collective vision of the school community if sustainability is to be achieved.

Taking a systemic approach does not mean that a school's systems are so rigid that adapting to new challenges is impossible. Systems without flexibility can be worse than no systems at all. Systems must be dynamic and flexible enough to adapt to the long line of inevitable challenges each new educational initiative is sure to bring with it.

SELF-RENEWAL

> *Wanted: A miracle worker who can do more with less, pacify rival groups,
> endure chronic second-guessing, tolerate low levels of support, process large
> volumes of paper and work double shifts (75 nights a year out). He or she will
> have carte blanche to innovate, but cannot spend much money, replace any
> personnel, or upset any constituency.*

—Robert Evans

The principal is a school resource, and as such the principal ought to view her or himself as a renewable resource. This concept is easily grasped, but difficult for principals to adopt in the face of increasing demands and growing job complexity.

Principals often see their roles as the school's ombudsman who is the one who has to be all things to all people. A principal taking time for him or herself is not selfish; actually, quite the opposite is true. It is the height of unselfishness to take time to renew oneself to be of better service to others. Renewing oneself comes in many forms and is both a personal and professional necessity. This is a philosophy that those in the principalship appear to espouse for everyone else but him or herself.

Principals have to step off of the treadmill from time to time to reassess their needs if they hope to be able to effectively continue to assess the needs of the school. Heifetz (1994) uses the phrase *finding a sanctuary* to describe the leader's need to remove her or himself from the cacophony and "restore one's sense of purpose, put issues in perspective, and regain courage and heart" (p. 272). Heifetz recognized that the leader serves "as the repository of many conflicting aspirations" (p. 272), and in this role a person can lose her or himself "by failing to distinguish his inner voice from the voices that clamor for attention outside" (p. 272).

Hargreaves and Fink (2004) suggest that "most leaders want to do things that matter, to inspire others to do it with them, and to leave a legacy once they have gone" (p. 13) and this is accomplished when leaders can "develop sustainability by how they approach, commit to, and protect deep learning in their schools" (p. 13). Hargreaves and Fink were quick to recognize that "even the most motivated and committed leaders can only sustain themselves for so long" (p. 12) and point to distributing leadership and responsibilities to others as key factors in leaders' ability to sustain themselves and avoid burnout.

Peters (2011) points out that it is critically important, now more than ever, "to establish and maintain a process to support and sustain school leaders" (p. 68) because what was once a stable profession has devolved to become a revolving door.

Hargreaves and Fink (2004) offer seven benefits to implementing a sustainable leadership approach:

1. Sustainable leadership creates and preserves sustaining learning.
2. Sustainable leadership secures success over time.
3. Sustainable leadership sustains the leadership of others.
4. Sustainable leadership addresses issues of social justice.
5. Sustainable leadership develops rather than depletes human and material resources.
6. Sustainable leadership develops environmental diversity and capacity.
7. Sustainable leadership undertakes activist engagement with the environment.

A sustainable culture requires principals to practice what they preach and model self-renewal for emerging teacher-leaders. The act of leading is more than a string of connected decisions and directives; "leadership is as much a spiritual connection to the hearts of people as it is a managerial concern about professional performance" (Jansen, 2005, p. 204). The principal's ability to make meaningful connections and see the larger long-term picture is dependent on not getting stuck in the quagmire of administrative minutia. If the leader is "preoccupied with narrow administrative tasks, the cost is huge in terms of the broader strategic and positioning functions . . ." (p. 204).

If principals and teacher-leaders do not practice self-renewal, what is the alternative? Leaders who are eventually used up, sucked dry, and run down will be in no condition to serve their schools well. The leader whose internal wellspring is at risk of drying up will instinctively turn his or her attention to less emotionally draining administrative tasks and, in doing so, can lose the big-picture perspective.

Building time for principals to self-renew or *sharpen the saw* is not a new concept. *Sharpening the saw* was the phrase used by Covey (1989) as a practice found commonly among highly effective people. Sharpening the saw speaks to how we can sustain ourselves over the long haul. Leading a school is much more like a marathon than a sprint; it needs to be viewed this way. Immediate short-term successes at the cost of sustainable long-term successes may help a short-timer springboard to another school or gain a promotion to a central office position, but short-term gains are short-sighted and will ultimately make sustaining a culture many times more difficult for the teacher-leaders and their next principal.

Focusing exclusively on the immediate satisfaction of short-term goals at the cost of long-term goals is shortsighted and will ultimately do more harm than good. Farmland is treated sustainably when farmers expect the farm will be passed on to their descendants and thriving long after they are gone. Another word for the action of caring for something and making it better until it is passed on might be *stewardship*. School cultures are treated sustainably when principals act as stewards who expect the culture to be thriving long after their tenure. A vibrant sustainable culture is potentially the most powerful legacy and greatest gift a principal can leave to a school community.

Covey (1989) suggests that highly effective people spend a minimum of one hour a day developing their physical, spiritual, and mental dimensions. Covey explains that one's economic security does not reside in one's job, but rather in one's ability to think, to learn, to create, and adapt. Covey makes the distinction between possessing wealth and possessing the power to produce wealth. Principals can make a similar distinction between leading a school and possessing the ability to have a school well-led. In the same way that financial security is not about having wealth, as fortunes are lost every day, school leadership is not about the formal leadership invested in the principal, it is about the school community's capacity to think, to learn, to create, and adapt. Distributive leadership is an adaptation which, once embraced by the principal, can transform a school.

Murphy, Smylie, Mayrowetz, and Louis (2009) liken the ability to have the school well-led to the principal being in the role of theatre director. "The research is clear that it is the principal who needs to set the stage for the distributed leadership play to be successfully enacted" (p. 193). The distinction is that the principal does not have to be an actor for a successful play; he or she needs to "set the stage" for others to find success. Effective school cultures support the concept that "teacher leadership is neither in conflict nor in competition with the idea of administrative leadership" (Danielson, 2006, p. 18).

The formal leadership role held by the principal is critical to the success or failure of both restructuring and reculturing the school. Murphy et al. (2009) recognized that "all change flows through the principal's office" (p. 181), and as formal leader of the school, principals "are in a critical position to move initiatives forward or to kill them off, quickly through actions or slowly through neglect. This law of change is magnified in the area of distributed leadership" (p. 181).

The time for principals to start thinking about their succession plan is even before they first move into the principal's office. Thinking about succession planning right before the principal plans to move on is often too late. Principals who desire sustainable change incorporate keeping the end in mind with each step along the way. Every decision the principal makes is an opportunity to build a sustainable system that will not be killed off quickly through actions or slowly through neglect once the current principal moves on. The new principals are simultaneously juggling three balls: past, present, and future. New principals will ask themselves:

- How can I preserve and sustain what was good about the previous administration, so the teachers are not starting from scratch?
- With that in mind, how can I build upon what has been done in a sustainable way and add to it?
- At some point in the future another principal will be in my shoes; how can what I pass along be made sustainable?

The traditional approach to the principalship is being reinvented in many schools. The rise of distributed leadership "as a powerful concept and a theory represents a significant shift in thinking about leaders, leadership, and leadership development. It not only challenges the mythology of individualistic leadership but also reclaims leadership for teachers and others working in schools" (Harris, 2005, p. 262). School transformation is seen as inseparable from principal transformation. Murphy et al. (2009) suggest that "the message to be underscored here is that for many principals a personal transformation in leadership must accompany the quest to rebuild schooling to cultivate distributed leadership and efforts to nurture the growth of teacher leaders" (p. 183). In short, a principal cannot make a long-term positive impact on a school's culture if he or she is not willing to be changed.

SERVANT LEADERSHIP

Once the principal is in a position to serve the school as a renewable resource, he or she can become that resource through servant leadership. Robert Greenleaf is credited with coining the term *servant leadership* in 1970 (van Dierendonck, 2011; Hu & Liden, 2011). Servant leadership is characterized by being the servant first and the leader second. Many parents instinctively practice servant leadership; they are in charge of their children, but put their own interests second to those of their children. Servant leadership is what occurs in schools when a principal embraces teacher leadership, puts aside self-interests, and fosters followers to achieve objectives beneficial to their career goals.

In a 2007 study by Hale and Fields (as cited in Walumbwa, Hartnell, & Oke, 2010), servant leadership was defined as "an understanding and practice of leadership that places the good of those led over the self-interest of the leader, emphasizing leader behaviors that focus on follower development, and de-emphasizing the glorification of the leader" (p. 397). It may take principals some practice to build the skill necessary to genuinely place the good of those led over the self-interest of the leader. Jones (2011) stated that "servant leaders encourage the elements of care, trust, collaboration, listening, foresight, empowerment, and positive ethical use of their power . . ." (p. 21). In a 2011 study examining the impact of servant leadership on team effectiveness and potency, Hu and Liden suggest that leaders will need to learn to develop certain behaviors. These behaviors that require training include performing ethically and empowering others. In order to fully develop teacher-leaders, principals have to increasingly empower them with the autonomous authority to make meaningful decisions and not simply delegate low-level tasks. This skill, along with performing ethically, as can be inferred from Hu and Liden, may need to be learned.

Walumbwa et al. (2010) describe the servant leader as "attentive to their followers' personal development through understanding their existing skills, knowledge, needs, goals, and abilities" (p. 519). Servant leadership is more than empowering others; it involves making a leadership paradigm shift. Denhardt and Denhardt (2000) suggest that "public administrators must not only share power, work through people, and broker solutions, they must reconceptualize their role in the governance process as a responsible participant . . ." (p. 557).

If the first step is understanding that followers need to become teacher-leaders in more than name only, the next step is supporting emergent teacher-leaders to reach those goals. Servant leaders create opportunities for their followers to develop new skills that will assist them reaching their career goals. "Therefore, such leaders are more likely to enable their followers to be successful by developing and improving their repertoire of skills, knowledge, and abilities, thereby increasing self-efficacy" (p. 519). Starratt (2004a) offers responsibility, authenticity, and presence as three virtues necessary to "infuse and energize the work of schools and hence the work of school leaders in schools" (p. 9).

Walumbwa et al. (2010) identified the three dimensions of servant leadership as:

1. A moral component
2. Uniquely concerned with the success of all organizational stakeholders
3. Focused on followers' individual growth and development (acting in the best interest of the follower)

In the same way that only by stepping out of the comfort of the nest can a fledgling bird ever hope to soar, it is only by stepping out of the relative security of the traditional role of principal that a sustainable culture supportive of teacher leadership can be established. This is likely to be very uncomfortable for those wedded to the traditional connotation of principal as sole superleader for the school.

SUSTAINABILITY

Sustainability is defined by Early (as cited by Bartuska & Kazimee, 2005) as a process that "integrates natural systems with human patterns and celebrates continuity, uniqueness and placemaking" (p. 221). Change is relatively easy to create, but much more difficult to create sustainably. As Covey (2008) warned leaders, "the real challenge is not in creating change as much as it is in sustaining change. Any principal will tell you, for example, that it is far easier to jump to higher test scores than it is to sustain those scores" (p. 185).

Sustainability is impossible if those in the school do not know in which direction they are individually and collectively headed. Covey and Gulledge (1992) suggests leaders try an experiment in which, without warning, you ask people at your next meeting to close their eyes and point north. This activity is designed to show that while everyone may be doing their best, they all have a different perception of which way is *true north*. True north for Covey is a metaphor for a set of principles that can serve as one's guiding compass, allowing effective people to prioritize according to their values and not simply be driven by a schedule. Becoming driven by a schedule is a real concern for principals with full calendars.

Principals will need to enlist the help of their secretaries and staff if they hope to not be driven by, or as is often the case run over by, their schedules. If the secretary, who is responsible for keeping the principal's calendar, schedules with an intentionality of meeting established goals, then the principal's job will become more sustainable. The way the formal leader spends her or his time, and with whom, has a profound influence on the effectiveness of the school. Principals can stop, or at the very least reduce being driven by a busy schedule and start driving their schedules to accomplish school goals.

When appointments are made and time set aside to accomplish tasks in alignment with an established set of priorities, the principal can manage her or his time much more efficiently. Taking charge of how a principal spends time requires empowering the principal's secretary to make scheduling decisions in the same way a triage nurse decides what needs the doctor's immediate attention and what can wait. Informing the staff of the rationale behind the change is critical to its success. Principals who prioritize how they spend their time will not allow others to dictate the principal's priorities. Effectiveness and efficiency dramatically increase when principals become proactive as opposed to being reactive. Drop-in visits that are not urgent do not necessitate changing set priorities for the day, and as such are instead rescheduled for a more conducive time.

How the principal spends her or his time is directly correlated to the principal's priorities. The principal who spends the most time on goals of the highest priority, and the second-most time on goals of the second-highest priority, etc., will find over time that intentionality pays off. The converse is often the case for principals who are over-scheduled because they spend the majority of their time on activities that have little or no bearing on their long-term goals. Principals who value fostering teacher-leaders regularly schedule activities that support that goal, and this time is held sacrosanct.

Hargreaves and Goodson (2006), as cited in Danielson (2006), emphasized the distinction between institutionalizing changed practices and actually creating a culture that critically examines daily practices. The distinction between the former and the latter is key to creating sustainable educational change. One institutionalizes a route, while the other teaches how to read a map. Creating a culture that critically examines practices ensures that those in the school will possess the skillset necessary to adapt and find new routes when roadblocks are encountered. Fullan (2005) found that when district leaders understand "the change process and the corresponding capacity-building, they appreciate what needs to be done" (p. 213). Fullan identified *what needs to be done* as supporting professional learning communities by creating systems to foster "a collective moral purpose, organize the structure and roles most effectively, provide ongoing leadership development for those in key roles, and formulate strategies where schools learn from each other (lateral capacity-building)" (p. 213).

Providing ongoing leadership development for those in key roles is accomplished through cross-pollination among educational professionals. Fullan (2005) suggests that lateral capacity building or schools sharing information to help each other find their way can be accomplished through professional learning communities.

Giles and Hargreaves (2006) identified three roadblocks to sustainable change in schools, one of which is a roadblock to lateral capacity building. The three common forces standing in the way of the sustainability of innovative efforts were identified as: envy and anxiety among competing institutions in the surrounding system; the evolutionary process of aging and decline in the organizational lifecycle; and the regressive effects of large-scale, standardized reform strategies (p. 127). Giles and Hargreaves suggest that the future of learning organizations depends, in part, on the capacity to teach schools to "learn how to halt the evolutionary attrition of change by renewing their teacher cultures, distributing leadership, and planning for leadership succession" (p. 152).

Fullan (1998) calls for reshaping school leadership for the 21st century and stresses that school leaders break the bonds of dependency. Dependency, Fullan explains, comes in two interrelated conditions: 1) over-burdened principals who 2) must resort to limiting packaged solutions. He describes the job of the principal as having become increasingly complex and constrained. "Principals find themselves locked in with less and less room to maneuver" (p. 6). When principals are barraged day after day by "disjointed demands," it creates dependency on pre-packaged solutions. Fullan warns that boxing in principals puts them in the least favorable position to provide what is most needed, which is proactive leadership. Principals "need a new mindset and guidelines for action to break through the bonds of dependency that have entrapped those who want to make a difference in their schools" (p. 6).

Fullan (1998) advises principals that there are no silver bullet solutions, and the sooner they stop searching in vain for one, the sooner they can begin overcoming dependency and start taking actions that matter. Abandoning the fallacy of a silver bullet "frees educational leaders to gain truly new insights that can inform and guide their actions toward greater success, mobilizing resources for teaching and learning with children as the beneficiaries" (p. 7). Fullan states that when principals come to the realization that no magic answer exists, it "can be quite liberating. Instead of hoping that the latest technique will at last provide the answer, we approach the situation differently. Leaders for change get involved as learners in real reform situations" (p. 7).

Hargreaves and Fullan (1998) offer four guidelines to help principals reshape leadership:

1. ***Respect those you want to silence***—recognizing that resistance to initiative can be highly instructive.
2. ***Move toward the danger in forming new alliances***—principals must realize that school reform goes hand-in-hand with community reform. Schools cannot compartmentalize meeting student's needs; it must be done in conjunction with the broader community.
3. ***Manage emotionally as well as rationally***—"Reculturing, because it is based on relationships, requires strong emotional involvement from principals and others. It also pays emotional dividends. It contributes to personal and collective resilience in the face of change" (Fullan, 1998, p. 9).
4. ***Fight for lost causes (be hopeful when it counts)***—Hopeful principals rebound quicker from bad days and are less likely to succumb to the daily stresses of the job because they possess a better perspective.

DIFFERING PERSPECTIVES MAKE FOR A STRONGER SHARED VISION

A scene familiar to those who watch wildlife documentaries about life on the African plains is that of a gazelle being chased by a cheetah across the plains only to run smack into a tree. The reason is not that the gazelle is blinded by fear, but rather that it has a vastly different field of vision than a human, or even a cheetah, for that matter. Gazelles can see much farther back along each side of their head, approximately 35° farther. This makes it difficult for predators to sneak up behind them. The tradeoff for this beneficial adaptation is that gazelles sacrifice a good deal of depth perception. Humans and chee-tahs, on the other hand, have binocular vision, with two eyes set apart in the front of our heads. The visual data sent to our brains can be interpreted to provide information about the relative distances of objects that is much better than the data sent to the gazelle's brain.

In a school with a shared vision differing perspectives are not only tolerated, they are encouraged. In the same way two eyes with different perspectives can provide the brain with superior data to create depth perception, the school in which teacher-leaders possess differing views from each other and their principal are best positioned to meet their common goal. Schools benefit from the interpretation of multiple perspectives.

Contrast a multiple perspective school with a school where the leaders discourage differing views. If the principal only tolerates one "right way" to achieve the school's com-mon vision, those in that school might find that this lack of perspective, not unlike the gazelle, causes them to run into unseen obstacles. Lacey (2003) warns that when leaders are left to their own informal processes, they have a tendency to create a monocular vision. Principals tend to select "those future potential leaders that most closely reflect their own values, experiences and attitudes . . ." (p. 7). This kind of insular thinking can create an organization with a very narrow perspective. It is important for principals to recognize the distinction between a common or shared vision and monocular vision.

SUCCESSION PLANNING

Lacey (2003) found that in addition to ensuring that their "human resource practices sup-port the recruitment, development, and retention of appropriate leadership personnel, organizations must include" (p. 1) effective succession planning. Succession planning has taken on importance beyond merely planning for replacing those who leave or retire. Succession planning ensures that the common vision and goals of the school will not change with every new principal, but that instead new principals will be recruited who possess a similar educational and philosophical ideology as the school community. "Fail-ure to care for leadership succession is sometimes a result of manipulation or self-cen-teredness; but more often it is oversight, neglect, or the pressures of crisis management that are to blame" (Hargreaves, 2005, p. 167).

A study by Peters (2011) of succession planning in an urban district found that despite principals playing "a central role in ensuring organizational success . . . they play little or no role in the selection of their successors or in the transition process" (p. 65). A majority of school districts "do not incorporate succession planning into an overall school improvement plan, and leader succession is often an effort to move schools in a different direction and not maintain a continuity with the existing culture established by the exiting school leader" (p. 69). This could be countered by proactive succession planning, which "increases its effectiveness when schools distribute leadership beyond that authority of one individual" (p. 67). Peters also found that the resulting collaboration "provides teachers and members of the school community ownership and investment in the organization, which assists in sustaining much of the progress made from leader to leader. Debunking the notion of "superleader" who acts alone as a change agent . . ." (p. 67).

It stands to reason that the more leadership is distributed throughout a school, the more sustainable the culture will be when one of its leaders leaves, even if that leader is the principal. Harris (2005) found that distributing leadership, knowledge, and expertise makes an organization less vulnerable to shifts and changes. Collective expertise was found "less likely to be destabilized by external or internal changes as the knowledge is broadly based" (p. 262). Distributed leadership was found to ensure that professional development "is naturally built into the system: the overlapping areas of expertise and collaborative ways of working create a powerful learning environment . . ." (p. 262). Distributed leadership was also discovered to be "more likely to result in long-term system stability and continuity of school performance; there is an inherent mechanism of adjustment and adaptation built in through members sharing expertise" (p. 262).

THE FRUITS OF PRINCIPAL ROBERTA'S SUSTAINABILITY PLANNING

Principal Roberta eventually moved beyond transformational leadership, with its aim to align the leader's "own and others' interests with the good of the group" (Parolini, Patterson, & Winston, 2009, p. 274), and into servant leadership, with an aim of "selecting the needs of others and serving others as the leader's main aim" (p. 274). Roberta made a concerted effort to learn the aspirations of her staff and actively sought ways help them flourish.

Roberta transformed the teacher evaluation process from a perceived "gotcha" at worst or bureaucratic hoop to jump through at best into a collaborative process about professional growth and development. Areas of weakness became improvement goals, and strengths were seen as opportunities to nudge teachers into formal and informal leadership positions.

Roberta created a culture of trust that supported teachers following their passions: six teachers expanded their horizons to instruct part-time at local colleges; three teachers became educational authors; one went on to become a principal of her own school following a principal internship with Roberta; three became educational consultants and travel around the country; one became state teacher of the year; and another became a semi-finalist for teacher of the year.

Roberta was persistent in spite of frequent criticism early on for having too many committees and teacher teams. She was questioned about why she did not just make the decisions: "Isn't that what you're paid to do?" It took a few years for the teachers to appreciate the wisdom in Roberta's approach. Teachers slowly became more invested, assuming teacher-leader roles, and cannot now imagine a system where they would not have significant involvement in the decision-making process. Roberta always gave credit where it was due; she sought to be viewed as a coach on the sidelines and not a star on the field.

Surrendering the traditional approach to the principalship and distributing leadership has made Roberta far more influential a school leader than she ever could have become if she had not invested leadership in teachers. Roberta's school abounds with teacher-leaders who pursue their passions and are trusted to make significant school decisions. The school thrives because almost all the teachers are invested in its success. Teachers' investment in the school means that "not my job" is seldom uttered. Working together to make the school the best that it can be is seen as everyone's job. The high level of teacher job satisfaction makes it a happier place for students to learn. The school culture has become a self-fulfilling cycle. Educators give more of themselves and enjoy their time at work because they find a lot of fulfillment in their jobs and in interacting with optimistic colleagues; at the same time, working in an environment where colleagues enjoy their work encourages educators to give more of themselves and go that extra mile.

Roberta's school enjoys a strong reputation for its positive culture among area teachers. When a teaching position vacancy occurs, the office is overrun with applications from teachers in neighboring communities who have been biding their time for the chance to interview at Roberta's school. It is mostly through word of mouth from current teachers that potential candidates have learned about the school's supportive culture of empowering teachers. The current teachers are highly invested in preserving their positive culture, and as such the interviewing process is intensive. Teachers want to replace those leaving with individuals who will add to and not detract from the school's culture.

Roberta will be the first to admit that it is not all puppies and rainbows at her school. She puts in many long hours, and struggles with complexities that are the reality of a modern principalship, including the challenge to improve student results on state test scores. Like every principal, she has days when it seems the fates have conspired to gang up on her. Roberta's school will never stop working to improve. Roberta says, "There is no finish line in school improvement."

Roberta and the teacher-leaders are working to build a greater capacity for colleague-to-colleague difficult conversations. Roberta recognizes how difficult it is for teachers, who make a living offering constructive criticism to students, to give or receive criticism when the other person is an adult. Shifting the focus of difficult discussions from *what is taught* to *what is learned* and from *practitioner* to *practice* has helped.

The difference between Roberta and principals in schools without thriving distributive leadership cultures is that she does not face these struggles alone; she can let her guard down because she works with a faculty that has her back covered, as she has their backs. The principal, teacher-leaders, and teachers feel their work together can be tough, but it remains meaningful. Roberta often paraphrases Rick Warren (2002) when people talk about how much hard work is involved in leading a school: "It is usually meaningless work, not overwork, that wears us down, saps our strength, and robs our joy." The teacher-leaders in Roberta's school work hard, but the resulting culture energizes and fulfills them.

In Summary

As counterintuitive as it may seem, successful schools abandon the notion that only one person can lead a school, and by "empowering others to make significant decisions" (Leithwood & Riehl, 2003, p. 5) make it possible for principals to bring about the goals they seek. Leithwood and Riehl capture the new thinking about school leaders when they describe them as those persons "occupying various roles in the school, who provide direction and exert influence in order to achieve the school's goals" (p. 1) and characterize formal leaders by saying "Those persons in formal positions of authority are genuine leaders only to the extent that they fulfill these functions" (p. 1).

Being the leader of leaders means looking at teachers in the school through a different lens. Sustainability comes from recognizing and building the leadership capacity in others. Teacher leadership will take on as many different forms as there are teacher-leaders; no two leadership styles are identical. The school that expects differing views and encourages difficult conversations, instead of shying away from them, will be better positioned to build a dynamic, resilient culture.

There is no one best model to fit all schools, no single roadmap that will guide principals to a culture supportive of teacher leadership, and no quick fixes when reculturing a school. As Leithwood and Riehl (2003) point out, "leadership functions can be carried out in many different ways, depending on the individual leader, the context, and the nature of the goals being pursued" (p. 1). Creating a culture is less than half the battle; sustaining it is where the real work begins.

Student achievement, the holy grail in this current era of accountability, is actually a by-product of effective school cultures. Schools where the moral and ethical needs of students and staff are paramount and where teachers share in leadership responsibilities and make contributions beyond their formal job requirements cannot help but have a positive impact on school culture and in doing so positively impact student achievement.

Chapter Discussion Questions

1. Identify three areas where you can genuinely place the good of those you lead over your own self-interests. List the potential benefits for each area identified.
2. Would the members of your school community agree on true north? Is everyone in the school using the same guiding compass? If not, what steps could you take to align values and set common priorities?
3. Does your school suffer from monocular vision? When are differing views discouraged, tolerated, or encouraged? Provide an example for each.
4. Would the culture in your school survive the unsuspected departure of the principal? If not, what steps could be taken to build a succession plan now? If so, what steps are in place supporting the succession plan?

CONCLUSION

To traditionalists, teacher leadership challenges the hierarchal structure of schools; it allocates leadership to those traditionally considered followers. More and more, however, it is becoming clear that both principals *and* teachers can lead, and that the profession in general and teaching and learning in particular can benefit as a result. Basic to the successful and effective implementation of shared leadership are a) the purposeful undertaking by the principal of the role of leader of leaders and b) the culture, climate, and structure that support and nourish emergent and active teacher leadership.

In the role of leader of leaders, the principal recognizes that no one person in the building is the most knowledgeable or experienced in all of its aspects. Rather, the principal honors and encourages the strengths of the staff and taps into each member's expertise to improve teaching and learning in the school. The principal works ethically with the staff to develop a strong professional culture in which teachers continuously collaborate and are supported in their leadership aspirations and endeavors.

According to the Center for Collaborative Education (2001), the leader of leaders' role focuses on five interconnected areas (p. 13):

1. Sharing real decision-making power with staff and faculty by providing meaningful opportunities for teachers to participate in significant decision making.
2. Providing support for effective functioning of teams by ensuring that teachers have the skills and understanding to participate effectively in those teams.
3. Regularly visiting classrooms to work with teachers and students, or attending academic team meetings to assist the development of effective teaching and learning strategies.
4. Developing collaborative accountability by holding individuals and teams accountable for reaching their goals.
5. Managing and monitoring the change process to make sure it is always moving forward.

Like Roberta, the principal whose story is detailed throughout this book, Bonnie Wilson, Principal of Baldwin Academy, a K-5 elementary school in La Puente, California, exemplifies these attributes. Wilson develops leaders out of the majority of her staff by seeking out each staff member's strengths and providing them with leadership opportunities in those particular areas. After every professional development training session, each staff member commits to one thing he or she will do in the next 24 hours, and then the grade-level teams help and assist each other to address their commitment. Wilson then goes around to classes encouraging and monitoring what was done in professional development to make sure it is implemented in each classroom. In addition, teachers regularly visit each other's classrooms, demonstrate lessons, and share best practices.

Wilson identifies the elements of Baldwin's culture that supports teacher collaboration and leadership as follows:

- All teachers work together in grade-level teams, share ideas, and visit each other's classes.
- There is nothing that teachers can't ask Wilson or another colleague for help with.
- All data is shared and analyzed together because that way teachers can see how they can get help from someone else on their team.

- Each grade level team picks a team leader every year who sits on the school's leadership team.
- There are high expectations for implementation of staff development and grade level decisions.
- The staff lead trainings and share all ideas with others in the school.
- There is continuous development of teacher-leaders as they take over areas of the school, such as the development of curriculum and student grading policies.

The culture and activities that take place at Baldwin Academy could not have happened without a foundation of openness and trust. Over the years, teachers have experienced that their principal views leadership as a collaborative process, and that she respects and honors their decisions.

HOW DO WE KNOW IF TEACHER LEADERSHIP IS WORKING?

Cortez-Ford (2006) contends that principals and teachers who have worked hard to create structures and processes of teacher leadership realize that "gut feelings" are not enough to fully understand whether their efforts have been effective. But how can they assess their efforts in order to ensure that teacher leadership is supporting the achievement of their goals? The answer, Cortez-Ford suggests, lies in the data. A school's ability to improve is dependent upon its ability to make data-based decisions. Perception data is particularly useful in understanding how teacher leadership is working.

Perception data is significant in determining whether teacher leadership is working because it can provide valuable insight into how the members of the school community view its process, effectiveness, and value. It answers the question "How are we doing?" Perception data can be collected in a variety of ways, including surveys and questionnaires, individual or group interviews, and observation of teacher-leader activities.

It is also advantageous to consider perception data along with other data to get a clearer picture of the effectiveness of teacher leadership. For example, teacher leadership is an endeavor that supports student learning, school improvement, and instructional change. Look at the data using the perception lens first, and then look at it in relation to student achievement data. Questions to ask might include: "Are the students of teachers who perceive their instructional practices improved as a result of coaching performing better than students of teachers who are not being coached?" and "Are instructional practices improving as a result of coaching?"

Papay (2012) found evidence that gains in productivity associated with higher quality professional environments largely occur after teachers' first few years on the job, suggesting that teachers will continue to improve their instruction beyond these initial years when they work in an environment where the adults in the building share best practices and receive constructive feedback. Among the elements of the professional environment that appear to be the strongest predictors of student achievement is effective peer collaboration. The study used a comprehensive administrative dataset from Charlotte–Mecklenburg Schools (CMS), a large, urban school district located in North Carolina that includes student, teacher, and test records from the 2000–2001 to the 2009–2010 school years. Those data were combined with a rich set of school measures constructed from teachers' responses on a biannual survey of working conditions developed by Hirsch (2008) of The New Teacher Center.

WHY EVALUATE?

There are two compelling reasons to evaluate teacher leadership: for accountability (summative) and for improvement (formative). Evaluate for *accountability* in order to determine whether the program is reaching those whom it was designed to reach and is doing so in appropriate ways and times. Summative evaluation can also tell us teacher leadership's impact on school culture and its effect on student learning. Evaluate for *improvement* in order to determine what is and isn't working the way it is supposed to and why.

Assessment of teacher leadership is most effective when it is both formative and summative, and reflects an understanding of the process as multidimensional, integrated, and revealed over time. It involves not only knowledge and abilities, but also values, attitudes, and habits of mind that affect both outcomes and performance. Assessment works best when it is ongoing, not episodic. Though isolated, "one-shot" assessment can be better than none, both accountability and improvement are more likely to occur when assessment entails a linked series of activities undertaken over time.

Although there is some overlap between the two reasons for evaluating a program, let's look first at accountability.

Evaluating Teacher Leadership for Accountability

Decision makers want data that will help them determine whether the practice should be continued as is, expanded, cut back, or cut out. They are looking for evidence that the program is addressing its objectives and resulting in desired outcomes, and they want to be assured that they are getting their time and money's worth in the process. On another level, those closer to day-to-day operation and oversight of the program also want to be assured that "all systems are go," that everyone is doing what they are expected to do, and that they are doing it when and how they are supposed to.

Evaluation undertaken for purposes of accountability is descriptive. It delineates how things are now, perhaps how they have changed from the past, and possibly how they are expected to be in the future. The purpose of evaluation for accountability is to provide evidence that will have bearing on decisions about the program's continued existence.

Evaluating Teacher Leadership for Purposes of Improvement

Evaluating for purposes of *improvement* tends to be inferential. It involves what educators often refer to as formative evaluation. It looks at ways the various components of a program are being carried out, whether the ways they are being carried out are resulting in desired outcomes, and to what extent the components themselves are proving to be appropriate. It also attempts to capture and understand unexpected outcomes. Results are used to fine-tune or modify aspects of the program in order to make them more effective.

Data collected for purposes of accountability can also suggest areas needing improvement. For example, Ronfeldt, Loeb, and Wyckoff (2012) found, during a study of student achievement of over 850,000 New York City fourth- and fifth-grade students over 8 years, that students with a high turnover of teachers score lower in both English language arts and math than those with low teacher turnover rates. A question suggested as a result of this observation is, "If student achievement suffers from high teacher turnaround, how can teacher retention be increased?" Data suggests that one answer is mentoring by teacher-leaders as part of a comprehensive teacher induction and mentoring program.

In a critical review of 15 empirical studies conducted since the mid-1980s on the effects of support, guidance, and orientation programs—collectively known as induction—for beginning teachers, Ingersoll and Strong (2011) report that most of the studies reviewed provide empirical evidence for the claim that support and assistance for beginning teachers has a positive impact on three sets of outcomes: teacher commitment and retention, teacher classroom instructional practices, and student achievement.

Case in point: In 1998–1999, the Islip Public Schools on Long Island, New York retained only 29 (63%) of the 46 new teachers hired. Over the next 3 years, after instituting its induction and mentoring program, the district retained 65 (96%) of its 68 new hires. In addition to mentoring by trained teacher-leaders, the program featured collaborative study group activities and networking. The groups held sharing sessions in which teachers learned from and built respect for one another. Since the existence of Islip's induction program, evidence of their collaborative work can be seen in the number of students who earned a New York State Regents Diploma. At the end of the 2005–2006 school year, 97% of their graduating seniors earned a New York State Regents Diploma. The rate was 34% when they started their induction program.

It is the informal, open-ended kind of data gathering, however, that brings to the surface the unexpected happenings and subtle nuances that are a program's undercurrent of pressure points—the easily overlooked places where things are not what they had seemed at first blush. Structured interviews, observations, and surveys are the most common data-gathering methods used for evaluation, but how does one go about gathering the more elusive information that can be helpful for improving a program? People function differently when it comes to gathering information. Some go about it like Sherlock Holmes, for example, who operates in contrast to the styles of Dr. Watson and the detectives at Scotland Yard. While they zero in on the "obvious" suspect, and fit the evidence to justify their case, Holmes instead picks up on unusual facts and minute details, until he eventually builds a scenario that leads to the murder.

When gathering information for purposes of program improvement, don your double-visored Sherlock Holmes cap and activate your receptive information-gathering persona. Focus on details. Digest and ponder individual facts and clues without trying to fit them into any preconceived conceptual scheme. Be aware of the feel and inherent qualities of new information. Suspend judgment. Save your Dr. Watson style for accountability-focused evaluations.

THE BOTTOM LINE

The principalship has evolved in complexity over the last 50 years. Except possibly in the smallest schools, the era of the superleader has ended. Principals are not rulers; they are the leaders who must influence the hearts and minds of followers if they hope to reculture school leadership for the next 50 years. Principals whose actions are ethical and trustworthy can induce teachers "to perform actions above and beyond the line of duty, such as volunteering, exercising great endeavors or taking risks" (Popper, 2011, p. 29).

Ultimately, successful principals will be those who come to understand that teachers determine the culture and climate of the school and are better positioned to influence school improvement. Recognizing that teachers are closest to the classroom and the students, the effective principal understands that her or his role is that of leader of leaders. Leadership has to be shared with teachers in a culture that encourages and supports their development and activities. This may well be the mantra of such a school:

Our school is a community of teacher-leaders through which we empower our school, each other, and ourselves to succeed. Our culture of teacher-leaders has its roots in inquiry, not compliance; interdependence, not individualism; collaboration, not competition; and trust, not fear.

APPENDIX A

Suggested Reading for Those Interested in Additional Study about High-Performance Work Systems

Building High-Performance People and Organizations (2008) edited by Martha I. Finney. Praeger.

Good to Great (2001) by Jim Collins. HarperCollins.

High Performance Work Systems: The Digital Experience (1989) by David A. Buchanan and James McCalman. Routledge.

Learning from Saturn (2001) by Saul Rubinstein and Thomas Kochan. ILR Press.

Manufacturing Advantage: Why High Performance Work Systems Pay Off (2000) by Eileen Appelbaum, Thomas Bailey, Peter Berg, Arne L. Kalleberg. Cornell University Press.

Strategies for High Performance Organizations: The CEO Report (1998) by Edward E. Lawler III, Susan Mohrman, and Gerald Ledford, Jr. Jossey-Bass.

The Human Equation (1998) by Jeffrey Pfeffer. Harvard Business Review Press.

The New American Workplace (1994) by Eileen Applebaum and Rosemary Batt. Cornell University Press.

The Wisdom of Teams: Creating the High-Performance Organization (1993) by Jon R. Katzenbach and Douglas K. Smith. Harvard Business School Press.

Tomorrow's Organization: Crafting Winning Capabilities in a Dynamic World (1998) by Susan Mohrman, Jay Galbraith, and Edward E. Lawler III. Jossey-Bass.

APPENDIX B

Commission on Effective Teachers and Teaching

- **Ronarae Adams**, a National Board Certified Teacher (NBCT) program director at National University, from San Diego, CA.

- **Adele Bravo**, an elementary school teacher from Boulder, CO.

- **James Brooks**, a high school language and media arts teacher from Millers Creek, NC.

- **Andy Coons**, a middle school math teacher from Tacoma, WA.

- **Madaline Fennell** (chair), a fourth-grade elementary school teacher from Omaha, NE.

- **Sharon Gallagher-Fishbaugh**, president of the Utah Education Association, and a second-grade teacher from Salt Lake City, UT.

- **Michael Geisen**, a middle school science teacher from Prineville, OR.

- **Robert Goodman**, a math and science teacher from Teterboro, NJ.

- **Mary Hatwood-Futrell**, a professor of education from Washington, DC.

- **Malinda Ice**, a physical education teacher from St. Louis, MO.

- **Anne Keith**, a middle school math and communication arts teacher from Bozeman, MT.

- **Renee Moore**, a Mississippi Delta Community College English instructor from Moorhead, MS.

- **Shelly Moore**, a high school English and drama teacher from Ellsworth, WI.

- **Lori Nazareno**, a science teacher from Denver, CO.

- **Haydee Rodriguez**, a high school language, literature, and history teacher from El Centro, CA.

- **Kathleen Skinner**, director of the Center of Education Policy and Practice from Boston, MA.

- **Peggy Stewart**, a high school social studies teacher from Vernon, NJ.

- **Mary K. Tedrow**, a high school English teacher from Winchester, VA.

- **William Thomas**, a high school government teacher from Upper Marlboro, MD.

- **Andy Tompkins**, the president and CEO for the Kansas Board of Regents from Topeka, KS.

- **Kathleen Wiebke**, the executive director of Arizona K12 from Phoenix, AZ.

APPENDIX C

Teacher Leadership Exploratory Consortium

American Federation of Teachers

American Institutes for Research

Arkansas Department of Education

Bayonne Public Schools

Bethel College

Brandeis University

California Commission on Teacher Credentialing

Center for Teaching Quality

Council of Chief State School Officers

Dolphin Terrace Elementary School

Ysleta Independent School District

Edgar Allan Poe Middle School

San Antonio Independent School District

Texas Education Commission of the States

Educational Testing Service

Fairfax County School District

Georgia Professional Standards Commission

Harvard Graduate School of Education

Kansas State Department of Education

Kentucky Education Professional Standards Board

Learning Forward/National Staff Development Council

Malverne New York School District

Montclair State University

National Association of Elementary School Principals

National Education Association

New Jersey Department of Education

Ohio Department of Education

Oregon Teacher Standards and Practices Commission

Princeton University

State of Tennessee Board of Education

Temple University

The Danielson Group

University of Phoenix
Vernon Township New Jersey High School
Virginia Commonwealth University
Walla Walla Washington School District
Washington Professional Educator Standards Board
West Virginia Department of Education

APPENDIX D

Model Standards for Teacher Leadership

DOMAIN I

Fostering a collaborative culture to support educator development and student learning

The teacher leader is well versed in adult learning theory and uses that knowledge to create a community of collective responsibility within his or her school. In promoting this collaborative culture among fellow teachers, administrators, and other school leaders, the teacher leader ensures improvement in educator instruction and, consequently, student learning.

Functions

The teacher leader:

a. Utilizes group processes to help colleagues work collaboratively to solve problems, makes decisions, manages conflict, and promotes meaningful change;

b. **Models effective skills** in listening, presenting ideas, leading discussions, clarifying, mediating, and identifying the needs of self and others in order to advance shared goals and professional learning;

c. **Employs facilitation skills** to create trust among colleagues, develop collective wisdom, build ownership and action that supports student learning;

d. Strives to create an inclusive culture where diverse perspectives are welcomed in addressing challenges; and

e. **Uses knowledge and understanding of different backgrounds, ethnicities, cultures, and languages** to promote effective interactions among colleagues.

DOMAIN II

Accessing and using research to improve practice and student learning

The teacher leader keeps abreast of the latest research about teaching effectiveness and student learning, and implements best practices where appropriate. He or she models the use of systematic inquiry as a critical component of teachers' ongoing learning and development.

Functions

The teacher leader:

a. Assists colleagues in accessing and using research in order to select appropriate strategies to improve student learning;

b. Facilitates the analysis of student learning data, collaborative interpretation of results, and application of findings to improve teaching and learning;

c. Supports colleagues in collaborating with the higher education institutions and other organizations engaged in researching critical educational issues; and

d. Teaches and supports colleagues to collect, analyze, and communicate data from their classrooms to improve teaching and learning.

DOMAIN III

Promoting professional learning for continuous improvement

The teacher leader understands that the processes of teaching and learning are constantly evolving. The teacher leader designs and facilitates job-embedded professional development opportunities that are aligned with school improvement goals.

Functions

The teacher leader:

a. Collaborates with colleagues and school administrators to plan professional learning that is team-based, job-embedded, sustained over time, aligned with content standards, and linked to school/district improvement goals;

b. Uses information about adult learning to respond to the diverse learning needs of colleagues by identifying, promoting, and facilitating varied and differentiated professional learning;

c. Facilitates professional learning among colleagues; .

d. Identifies and uses appropriate technologies to promote collaborative and differentiated professional learning;

e. Works with colleagues to collect, analyze, and disseminate data related to the quality of professional learning and its effect on teaching and student learning;

f. Advocates for sufficient preparation, time, and support for colleagues to work in teams to engage in job-embedded professional learning;

g. Provides constructive feedback to colleagues to strengthen teaching practice and improve student learning; and

h. Uses information about emerging education.

DOMAIN IV

Facilitating improvements in instruction and student learning

The teacher leader possesses a deep understanding of teaching and learning, and models an attitude of continuous learning and reflective practice for colleagues. The teacher leader works collaboratively with fellow teachers to constantly improve instructional practices.

Functions

The teacher leader:

a. Facilitates the collection, analysis, and use of classroom- and school-based data to identify opportunities to improve curriculum, instruction, assessment, school organization, and school culture;

b. Engages in reflective dialog with colleagues based on observation of instruction, student work, and assessment data and helps make connections to research-based effective practices;

c. Supports colleagues' individual and collective reflection and professional growth by serving in roles such as mentor, coach, and content facilitator;

d. Serves as a team leader to harness the skills, expertise, and knowledge of colleagues to address curricular expectations and student learning needs;

e. Uses knowledge of existing and emerging technologies to guide colleagues in helping students skillfully and appropriately navigate the universe of knowledge available on the Internet, use social media to promote collaborative learning, and connect with people and resources around the globe; and

f. Promotes instructional strategies that address issues of diversity and equity in the classroom and ensures that individual student learning needs remain the central focus of instruction.

DOMAIN V

Promoting the use of assessments and data for school and district improvement

The teacher leader is knowledgeable about the design of assessments, both formative and summative. He or she works with colleagues to analyze data and interpret results to inform goals and to improve student learning.

Functions

The teacher leader:

a. Increases the capacity of colleagues to identify and use multiple assessment tools aligned to state and local standards;

b. Collaborates with colleagues in the design, implementation, scoring, and interpretation of student data to improve educational practice and student learning;

c. Creates a climate of trust and critical reflection in order to engage colleagues in challenging conversations about student learning data that lead to solutions to identified issues; and

d. Works with colleagues to use assessment and data findings to promote changes in instructional practices or organizational structures to improve student learning.

DOMAIN VI

Improving outreach and collaboration with families and community

The teacher leader understands the impact that families, cultures, and communities have on student learning. As a result, the teacher leader seeks to promote a sense of partnership among these different groups toward the common goal of excellent education.

Functions

The teacher leader:

a. Uses knowledge and understanding of the different backgrounds, ethnicities, cultures, and languages in the school community to promote effective interactions among colleagues, families, and the larger community;

b. Models and teaches effective communication and collaboration skills with families and other stakeholders focused on attaining equitable achievement for students of all backgrounds and circumstances;

c. Facilitates colleagues' self-examination of their own understandings of community culture and diversity and how they can develop culturally responsive strategies to enrich the educational experiences of students and achieve high levels of learning for all students;

d. Develops a shared understanding among colleagues of the diverse educational needs of families and the community; and

e. Collaborates with families, communities, and colleagues to develop comprehensive strategies to address the diverse educational needs of families and the community.

DOMAIN VII

Advocating for student learning and the profession

The teacher leader understands the landscape of education policy and can identify key players at the local, state, and national levels. The teacher leader advocates for the teaching profession and for policies that benefit student learning.

Functions

The teacher leader:

a. Shares information with colleagues within and/or beyond the district regarding how local, state, and national trends and policies can impact classroom practices and expectations for student learning;

b. Works with colleagues to identify and use research to advocate for teaching and learning processes that meet the needs of all students;

c. Collaborates with colleagues to select appropriate opportunities to advocate for the rights and/or needs of students, to secure additional resources within the building or district that support student learning, and to communicate effectively with targeted audiences such as parents and community members;

d. Advocates for access to professional resources, including financial support and human and other material resources, that allow colleagues to spend significant time learning about effective practices and developing a professional learning community focused on school improvement goals; and

e. Represents and advocates for the profession in contexts outside of the classroom.

Teacher Leadership Exploratory Consortium (2011). *Teacher leader model standards*. Retrieved from http://www.teacherleaderstandards.org/standards_overview

REFERENCES

Ackerman, R., & Mackenzie, S. V. (2006). Uncovering teacher leadership. *Educational Leadership 63*(8), 66–70.

Allen, R. (2005). *5-day brain compatible facilitator training: Presenting with the brain in mind*. San Diego, CA: The Brain Store.

Anderson, C., & Nesholm, K. (2010). *Inquiry-based science in Seattle preschools*. University of Illinois, Urbana-Champaign, College of Education, Early Childhood and Parenting Collaborative.

Anderson, M. G., & Iwanicki, E. F. (1984). Teacher motivation and its relationship to burnout. *Educational Administration Quarterly 20*(2), 109–132.

Anthony, N. (2006). From showpiece to learning hub. *Educational Leadership 63*(8). Retrieved from http://m.ascd.org/EL/Article/f1d808b4a ebfa010VgnVCM1000003d01a8c0RCRD

Ash, R. L., & Persall, M. (2000, May). The principal as chief learning officer: Developing teacher leaders. *NASSP Bulletin 84*(616), 15–22.

Barkley, S., Bottoms, G., Feagin, C. H., & Clark, S. (2001). *Leadership matters: Building leadership capacity*. Atlanta, GA: Southern Regional Educational Board.

Barnett, B. G., Basom, M. R., Yerkes, D. M., & Norris, C. J. (2000). Cohorts in educational leadership programs: Benefits, difficulties, and the potential for developing school leaders. *Educational Administration Quarterly 36,* 255–282.

Barth, R. S. (2001, February). Teacher leader. *Phi Delta Kappan 82*(6), 443–449.

Barth, R. S. (2007). The teacher leader. In R. H. Ackerman & S. V. Mackenzie (Eds.), *Uncovering teacher leaderships: Essays and voices from the field*. Thousand Oaks, CA: Corwin.

Bartuska, T. J., & Kazimee, B. A. (2005). Sustainable cells of urbanism: Regenerative theory and practice. M. Jenks & N. Dempsey (Eds.), *Future forms and design for sustainable cities*. Oxford: Architectural Press.

Bass, B. M. (1990). From transactional to transformational leadership: Learning to share the vision. *Organizational Dynamics 18*(3), 19–31.

Beck, L. G., & Murphy, J. (1993). *Understanding the principalship: Metaphorical themes 1920s–1990s*. New York, NY: Teachers College Press.

Berg, J. H., Charner-Laird, M., Fiarman, S. E., Jones, A., Qazilbash, E. K., & Johnson, S. M. (2005). *Cracking the mold: How second-stage teachers experience their differentiated roles*. Montreal, Canada: American Educational Research Association.

Berry, B. (2010). The coming age of the teacher-preneur. *Education Week*. Retrieved from http://www.edweek.org/tsb/articles/2010/10/ 12/01teacherpreneur.h04.html

Berry, B. (2011a). Moving past excuses: What excellence & equity require [Web log post]. Teacher Leader Network. Retrieved from http:// www.teachingquality.org/content/moving-past-excuses-what-excellence-equity-require

Berry, B. (2011b). *TEACHING 2030: What we must do for our students and our public schools . . . now and in the future*. New York, NY: Teachers College Press.

Bishop, J. (2007). *Increasing participation in online communities: A framework for human computer interaction*. Retrieved from http:// www.jonathanbishop.com/Web/Projects/ Publications/Display.asp?NoID=62$MID=9& NID=62&Item=17

Black, D. S. (2010). Defining mindfulness. *Mindfulness Research Guide*. Retrieved from http://www.mindfulexperience.org/

Black, G. L. (2010). Correlational analysis of servant leadership and school climate. *Catholic Education: A Journal of Inquiry and Practice 13*(4), 437–466.

Blase, J., & Blase, J. (2002). The dark side of leadership: Teacher perspectives of principal mistreatment. *Educational Administration Quarterly 38,* 671–727.

Blase, J., & Blase, J. (2006). *Teachers bringing out the best in teachers: A guide to peer consultation for administrators and teachers.* Thousand Oaks, CA: Corwin Press.

Boston Teacher Leadership Resource Center. (2012). *School conditions that support teacher leadership* [Draft]. Retrieved from http://www.bpe.org/teachers/teacherleaders

Boyd-Dimock, V., & McGree, K. M. (1995). Leading change from the classroom: Teachers as leaders: Issues about change. *SEDL* 4(4). Retrieved from http://www.sedl.org/change/issues/issues44.html#what-teacher-leaders-do

Braden, M. (2011). Preventing a leadership crash from overcorrecting [Web log post]. Retrieved from http://thoughtleadersllc.blogspot.com/2011/03/preventing-leadership-crash-from.html

Branstad, T. (2011). *Branstad-Reynolds administration blueprint unveils vision for Iowa's education remodel.* Retrieved from http://educateiowa.gov/index.php?option=com_content&view=article&id=2524:one-unshakeable-vision-world-class-schools-for-iowa&catid=830:department

Brubaker, D. L. (2004). *Revitalizing curriculum leadership: Inspiring and empowering your school community.* Thousand Oaks, CA: Corwin Press.

Burns, J. M. (1978). *Leadership.* New York, NY: Harper & Row.

Campbell, R. F., Fleming, T., Newell, L. J., & Bennion, J. W. (1987). *A history of thought and practice in educational administration.* New York, NY: Teachers College Press.

Casavant, C., Collins, W., Faginski, E., McCandless, J., & Tencza, M. (2012). *Perceptions of principal evaluation process and performance criteria: A qualitative study of the challenge of principal evaluation* (Doctoral dissertation, Boston College).

Center for Collaborative Education. (2001). *Guide to collaborative culture and shared leadership.* Retrieved from http://www.turningpts.org/pdf/Teams.pdf

Center for Comprehensive School Reform and Improvement. (2005). *What does the research tell us about teacher leadership?* (Research brief). Washington, DC: Author. Retrieved from http://www.centerforcsri.org/files/Center_RB_sept05.pdf

Center for Teaching Quality. (2011). *Checking in: What are teachers most excited about this year?* Retrieved from http://www.edweek.org/tm/articles/2011/09/07/link_checkingin.html

Chaskin, R. J. (2001). Defining community capacity: A definitional framework and case studies from a comprehensive community initiative. *Urban Affairs Review 36*(3), 291–323.

Clance, P. (1985). *The impostor phenomenon.* Atlanta, GA: Peachtree Publishers.

Clemson-Ingram, R., & Fessler, R. (1997, Fall). Innovative programs for teacher-leadership. *Action in Teacher Education 19*(3), 95–106.

Cody, A. (2009). Open letter to President Obama [Web log post]. Retrieved from http://blogs.edweek.org/teachers/living-in_dialogue/2009/11/open_letter_to_president_obama.html

Cohen, E., & Tichy, N. (1997, May). How leaders develop leaders. *Training & Development.* Retrieved from http://www.noeltichy.com/HowLeadersDevelopLeaders.pdf

Cohen, J., Fege, A., & Pickeral, T. (2009). Measuring and improving school climate: A strategy that recognizes, honors and promotes social, emotional and civic learning: The foundation for love, work and engaged citizenry. *Teachers College Record.* Retrieved from http://www.tcrecord.org/library/abstract.asp?contentid=15698

Cohen, J., McCabe, E. M., Michelli, N. M., & Pickeral, T. (2009). School climate: Research, policy, teacher education and practice. *Teachers College Record 111*(1), 180–213. Retrieved from http://www.tcrecord.org/Content.asp?ContentId=15220

Cortez-Ford, E. (2006). *Coaching teachers to be leaders.* Retrieved from http://www.educationworld.com/a_admin/columnists/cortez-ford/cortez-ford009.shtml

Cosner, S. (2009). Building organizational capacity through trust. *Educational Administration Quarterly 45,* 248–291.

Costa, A., & Kallick, B. (2000). *Habits of mind: A developmental series.* Alexandria, VA: Association for Supervision and Curriculum Development.

Covey, S. R. (1989). *The seven habits of highly effective people.* New York, NY: Simon & Schuster.

Covey, S. R. (2008). *The leader in me: How schools and parents around the world are inspiring greatness, one child at a time.* New York, NY: Simon & Schuster.

Covey, S. R., & Gulledge, K. A. (1992). Mission, vision and quality within organizations: Principle–centered leadership. *Journal for Quality and Participation 4,* 70–78.

Crevani, L., Lindgren, M., & Packendorff, J. (2010). Leadership, not leaders: On the study of leadership as practices and interactions. *Scandinavian Journal of Management 26,* 77–86.

Crews, A. C., & Weakley, S. (1995). *Hungry for leadership: Educational leadership programs in the SREB states.* Atlanta, GA: Southern Regional Education Board. (ERIC Document Reproduction Service No. ED391250)

Crowther, F. (1997). The William Walker oration, 1996: Unsung heroes: The leaders in our classrooms. *Journal of Educational Administration 35*(1), 5–17.

Danielson, C. (2006). *Teacher leadership that strengthens professional practice.* Alexandria, VA: Association for Supervision & Curriculum Development.

Danielson, C. (2007). The many faces of leadership. *Educational Leadership 65*(1), 14–19.

Davis, V. (2006). The classroom is flat. Teacherpreneurs and the Flat Classroom Project kickoff [Web log post]. Retrieved from http://coolcatteacher.blogspot.com/2006/11/classroom-is-flat-teacherpreneurs-and.html

Deal, T., & Peterson, K. D. (1999). *Shaping school culture: The heart of leadership.* San Francisco, CA: Jossey-Bass.

Denhardt, R., & Denhardt, J. (2000). The new public service: Serving rather than steering. *Public Administration Review 60,* 549–559.

Dimock, V., & McGree, K. (1995). Leading change from the classroom: Teachers as leaders. *Issues . . . about Change 4*(4). Retrieved from http://www.sedl.org/change/issues/issues44.html

Donaldson, G. A., Jr. (2007). What do teachers bring to leadership. *Educational Leadership 65*(1), 26–29.

DuFour, R. (2006, March). *Critical priorities in building a professional learning community.* Cybercast presentation to the Curriculum and Instruction Steering Committee of the California County Superintendents Educational Services Association.

Duignan, P. (2009). Educational leaders building innovating and deep-learning environments in schools. *Leading to Inspire.* Retrieved April 5, 2011, from http://www.cie.org.za/images/uploads/Leaders_Building_Deep_Learn_NOVEMBER_2009-1.pdf

Early, D. (1993). What is sustainable design? *The Urban Ecologist* (Spring), Society of Urban Ecology, Berkley.

Elmore, R. F. (2000). *Building a new structure for school leadership.* Washington, DC: Albert Shanker Institute.

Evans, R. (1995). Getting real about leadership. *Education Week 14*(29), 36.

Facilitator. (2013). In Merriam-Webster.com. Retrieved May 23, 2013, from http://www.merriam-webster.com/dictionary/facilitator

Fairman, J. C., & Mackenzie, S. V. (2012). Spheres of teacher leadership action for learning. *Professional Development in Education 38*(2), 229–246.

Fajans, F. (2000). Steering in bicycles and motorcycles. *American Journal of Physics 68*(7), 654–659.

Ferriter, B. (2012). What DOES teacher leadership look like in an #atplc school? [Web log post]. Retrieved from http://teacherleaders.typepad.com/the_tempered_radical/2012/08/teacherleadership-atplc-school.html#more

Fink, S., & Markholt, A. (2011). *Leading for instructional improvement.* San Francisco, CA: Jossey-Bass.

Floden, R. E., Goertz, M. E., & O'Day, J. (1995, September). Capacity building in systemic reform. *Phi Delta Kappan 77*(1), 19–21.

Forster, E. M. (1997). Teacher leadership: Professional right and responsibility. *Action in Teacher Education 19*(3), 82–94.

Fullan, M. (1997). The complexity of the change process. In M. Fullan (Ed.), *The challenge of school change* (pp. 33–56). Arlington Heights, IL: Skylight.

Fullan, M. (1998). Leadership for the twenty-first century. *Educational Leadership 55*(7), 6–11.

Fullan, M. G. (1999). *Change forces: The sequel.* Bristol, PA: Falmer Press.

Fullan, M. (2005). Professional learning communities writ large. In R. DuFour, R. Eaker, & R. DuFour (Eds.), *On common ground: The power of professional learning communities* (pp. 209–223). Bloomington, IN: National Educational Service.

Fullan, M. (2006). Leading professional learning: Think "system" and not "individual school" if the goal is to fundamentally change the culture of schools. *School Administrator 63*(10), 10–15.

Giles, C., & Hargreaves, A. (2006). The sustainability of innovative schools as learning organizations and professional learning communities during standardized reform. *Educational Administration Quarterly 42*(1), 124–156.

Glickman, C. (1989). Has Sam and Samantha's time come at last? *Educational Leadership 46*(8), 4–9.

Glover, E. (2007). Real principals listen. *Educational Leadership 65*(1), 60–63.

Goddard, R. D., & Goddard, Y. L. (2001). A multilevel analysis of teacher and collective efficacy. *Teaching and Teacher Education 17,* 807–818.

Goldring, E., Cravens, X. C., Murphy, J., Porter, A. C., Elliott, S. N., & Carson, B. (2009). The evaluation of principals: What and how do states and urban districts assess leadership? *The Elementary School Journal 110*(1).

Grammarist. (2012). Systematic vs. systemic. Retrieved from http://grammarist.com/usage/systematic-systemic/

Grant, C. (2008). "We did not put our pieces together": Exploring a professional development initiative through a distributed leadership lens. *Journal of Education 44,* 85–107.

Greenlee, B. J. (2007). Building teacher-leadership capacity through educational leadership programs. *Journal of Research for Educational Leaders 4*(1), 44–74.

Grossman, P., Wineburg, S., & Woolworth, S. (2000, December). *What makes teacher community different from a gathering of teachers?* Center for the Study of Teaching and Policy & Center on English Learning & Achievement (CELA), 49–53.

Hackney, C. E., & Henderson, J. G. (1999). Educating school leaders for inquiry-based democralearning communities. *Educational Horizons 77*(2), 67–73.

Hale, J. R., & Fields, D. L. (2007). Exploring servant leadership across cultures: A study of followers in Ghana and the USA. *Leadership 3,* 397–417.

Hallinger, P., & Heck, R. H. (2010). Collaborative leadership and school improvement: Understanding the impact on school capacity and student learning. *School Leadership & Management 30,* 95–110.

Hallinger, P., & Richardson, D. (1988). Models of shared leadership: Evolving structures and relationships. *The Urban Review 20,* 229–245.

Hargreaves, A. (2005). Leadership succession. *The Educational Forum 69*(2), 163–174.

Hargreaves, A., & Fink, D. (2004). The seven principles of sustainable leadership. *Educational Leadership 61*(7), 8–13.

Hargreaves, A., & Fullan, M. (1998). *What's worth fighting for out there?* New York, NY: Teachers College Press.

Hargreaves, A., & Goodson, I. (2006). Educational change over time? The sustainability and non-sustainability of three decades of secondary school change and continuity. *Educational Administration Quarterly 42*(1), 3–41.

Harms, P. D., & Credé, M. (2010). Emotional intelligence and transformational and transactional leadership: A meta-analysis. *Journal of Leadership and Organizational Studies 17,* 5–17.

Harris, A. (2003). Teacher leadership as distributed leadership: Heresy, fantasy or possibility? *School Leadership & Management 23*(3): 313–324.

Harris, A. (2005). Leading or misleading? Distributed leadership and school improvement. *Journal of Curriculum Studies 37*(3), 255–265.

Harris, A. (2008). Distributed leadership: According to the evidence. *Journal of Educational Administration 46,* 172–188.

Harris, A., & Lambert, L. (2003). *Building leadership capacity for school improvement.* Buckingham, UK: Open University Press.

Harris, A., & Muijs, D. (2005). *Improving schools through teacher leadership.* Berkshire, UK: Open University Press.

Harrison, C., & Killion, J. (2007). Ten roles for teacher leaders. *Educational Leadership 65*(1), 74–77.

Hattie, J. (2009). *Visible learning: A synthesis of over 800 meta-analyses relating to achievement.* Abingdon, Oxon, UK: Routledge.

Heck, R. H., & Hallinger, P. (2009). Assessing the contribution of distributed leadership to school improvement and growth in math achievement. *American Educational Research Journal 46,* 659–689.

Heifetz, R. (1994). *Leadership without easy answers.* Cambridge, MA: Harvard University Press.

Hill, M. S. (1995). Educational leadership cohort models: Changing the talk to change the walk. *Planning and Changing 26*(3/4), 179–189.

Hirsch, E. (2008). *Teacher working conditions: Setting the stage.* Retrieved from http://workingconditions.net/?p=105

Hirsh, S. (2011). *New teacher leader model standards released.* Retrieved from http://www.learningforward.org/about/news/5-6-2011TeacherLeaderPressRelease.cfm.gsu.edu/eps_diss/70

Hoffman, B. J., Bynum, B. H., Piccolo, R. F., & Sutton, A. W. (2011). Person-organization value congruence: How transformational leaders influence work group effectiveness. *Academy of Management Journal 54,* 779–796.

Hord, S. M., & Hirsh, S. A. (2009). The principal's role in supporting learning communities. *Educational Leadership 66*(5), 22–23.

Howey, K. R. (1988). Why teacher leadership? *Journal of Teacher Education 39*(1), 28–31.

Hoy, W. K., & Tarter, C. J. (2011). Positive psychology and educational administration: An optimistic research agenda. *Education Administration Quarterly 47,* 427–445.

Hu, J., & Liden, R. C. (2011). Antecedents of team potency and team effectiveness: An examination of goal and process clarity and servant leadership. *Journal of Applied Psychology 96*(4), 851–862.

Hulpia, H., Devos, G., & Van Keer H. (2011). The relation between school leadership from a distributed perspective and teachers' organizational commitment: Examining the source of the leadership function. *Educational Administration Quarterly 47*(5), 728–771.

Ingersoll, R., & Strong, M. (2011). The impact of induction and mentoring programs for beginning teachers: A critical review of the research. *Review of Education Research 81*(2), 201–233.

Interstate School Leaders Licensure Consortium (ISLLC) State Standards for School Leaders. (1996). Retrieved from http://soe.unc.edu/academics/requirements/standards/ISLLC_Standards.pdf

Jansen, J. D. (2005). The color of leadership. *The Educational Forum 69*(2), 203–211.

Johnson, S. M., & Donaldson, M. L. (2007). Overcoming the obstacles to leadership. *Educational Leadership 65*(1), 8–13.

Jones, M. F. (2011). *An examination of the meanings assigned to principal-teacher interaction and the relationship to school climate.* Unpublished doctoral dissertation, University of Alabama, Tuscaloosa.

Juechter, W. M., Fisher, C., & Alford, C. J. (1998). Five conditions for high-performance cultures. *Training & Development 52*(5), 63.

Juvonen, J. (2004). *Focus on the wonder years: Challenges facing the American middle school.* Prepared by the RAND Corporation. Arlington, VA: Edna McConnell Clark Foundation.

Kadela, S. (2009). Teacher leadership. *Quest Journal 61,* 1–11.

Katzenbach, J. R., & Smith, D. K. (2005). The discipline of teams. *Harvard Business Review 83*(7), 162.

Kelley, J. D. (2011). Teacher's and teacher leaders' perceptions of the formal role of teacher leadership. *Educational Policy Studies Dissertations*, Paper 70. Retrieved from http://digitalarchive.gsu.edu

Kelly, E. (2012, May). Why should teachers become teacher leaders? [Web log post]. Retrieved from http://blogs.edweek.org/teachers/leading_from_the_classroom/2012/05/why_should_teachers_become_teacher_leaders.html

Kelsey, K., Steel, A., & Steel, E. A. (2002). *The truth about science. A curriculum for developing young scientists.* Arlington, VA: NSTA Press.

Kempher, L., & Cooper, G. R. (2002). A document analysis of state-mandated principal evaluation programs in the north central association states. *Journal of School Business Management 14*(1), 30–35.

Knight, J. (2009). What can we do about teacher resistance? *Phi Delta Kappan 90,* 508–513.

Kollack, P. (1998). Social dilemmas: The anatomy of cooperation. *Annual Review of Sociology 24,* 183–214.

Kouzes, J. M., & Posner, B. Z. (2002). *The leadership challenge.* San Fransisco, CA: Jossey-Bass.

Kraus, C. M., & Cordeiro, P. A. (1995, October). *Challenging tradition: Re-examining the preparation of educational leaders for the workplace.* Paper presented at the annual meeting of the University Council for Educational Administration, Salt Lake City, UT. *Journal of Research for Educational Leaders 4*(1), 44–74. Retrieved from http://www.education.uiowa.edu/jrel

Krueger, J. A., & Milstein, M. M. (1995). Promoting excellence in educational leadership: What really matters? *Planning and Changing 26,* 148–167.

Lacey, K. (2003). *Succession planning in education.* Retrieved from http://www.apapdc.edu

Lambert, L. (2002). *Building leadership capacity in schools.* Retrieved from http://research.acer.edu.au/apc_monographs/2

Lambert, L. (2003). *Leadership capacity for lasting school improvement.* Alexandria, VA: Association for Supervision and Curriculum Development.

Lambert, L. (2005). What does leadership capacity really look like? *Journal of Staff Development, 26*(2), 38.

Lamoureax, K. (2009). Leaders teaching leaders: An important element of leadership development [Web log post]. Retrieved from http://www.bersin.com/blog/post/Leaders-Teaching-Leaders-An-Important-Element-of-Leadership-Development.aspx

Leadership Institute of Riverside County at the Riverside County Office of Education. (2012). *The Teacher Leader Certification Academy.* Retrieved from http://www.rcoe.k12.ca.us/leadershipinstitute/ on May 1, 2013.

Leana, C. R. (2011, Fall). The missing link in school reform. *Stanford Social Innovation Review 16.* Retrieved from http://www.ssireview.org/articles/entry/the_missing_link_in_school_reform

Leithwood, K., Harris, A., & Hopkins, D. (2008). Seven strong claims about successful school leadership. *School Leadership and Management 28*(1), 27–42.

Leithwood, K., & Mascall, B. (2008). Collective leadership effects on student achievement. *Educational Administration Quarterly 44*(4), 529–561.

Leithwood, K. A., & Riehl, C. (2003). *What we know about successful school leadership.* Philadelphia, PA: Temple University, Laboratory for Student Success. Retrieved from www.ncsl.org.uk/mediastore/image2/randd-leithwood-successful-leadership.pdf

Lieberman, A. (1992). Teacher leadership: What are we learning? In C. Livingston (Ed.), *Teachers as leaders: Evolving roles* (pp. 159–165). Washington, DC: National Education Association.

Linton, K. (2011). Living and learning in the 21st century [Web log post]. Retrieved from http://kirklintonblog.wordpress.com

Lipson, M. Y., Mosenthal, J. H., Mekkelsen, J., & Russ, B. (2004). Building knowledge and fashioning success one school at a time. *The Reading Teacher 57*(6), 534–542.

Livingston, C. (1992). Introduction: Teacher leadership for restructured schools. In C. Livingston (Ed.), *Teachers as leaders: Evolving roles.* NEA School Restructuring Series. Washington, DC: National Education Association.

Lord, B., & Miller, B. (2000*). Teacher leadership: An appealing and inescapable force in school reform?* Newton, MA: Education Development Center.

Loucks-Horsley, S., Hewson, P., Love, N., & Stiles, K. (1998). *Designing professional development for teachers of science and mathematics.* Thousand Oaks, CA: Corwin Press.

Louis, K., Leithwood, K., Wahlstrom, K., & Anderson, S. (2010). *Learning from leadership: Investigating the links to improved student learning.* Report commissioned by The Wallace Foundation. Retrieved from http://www.wallacefoundation.org/Pages/default.aspx

Lukwago, M. (2011). My style of teacher leadership. *Teacher Leader IV*(2). Retrieved from http://www.oakland.edu/upload/docs/GalileoNews/GalileoNewsVlIVI2.pdf

Mangin, M. M. (2005, July). Distributed leadership and the culture of schools: Teacher leaders' strategies for gaining access to classrooms. *Journal of School Leadership 15*(4), 456–484.

Margolis, J. M. (2010, April). *When leaders teach: The emergence of the hybrid teacher-leader amid complex professional development ecologies.* Paper presented at the annual meeting of the American Educational Research Association (AERA). Retrieved from the AERA Online Paper Repository, http://www.aera.net/Default.aspx?TabID=10250

Margolis, J., & Deuel, A. (2009). Teacher leaders in action: Motivation, morality, and money. *Leadership and Policy in Schools 8,* 264–286.

Marks, H. M., & Printy, S. M. (2003). Principal leadership and school performance: An integration of transformational and instructional leadership. *Educational Administration Quarterly 39*(3), 370–397.

Marks, M. A., Mathieu, J. E., & Zaccaro, S. J. (2000). A temporally based framework and taxonomy of team processes. *Academy of Management Review 26,* 356–376.

Marzano, R., Pickering, D., & Pollock, J. (2001). *Classroom instruction that works.* Alexandria, VA: Association for Supervision and Curriculum Development.

Marzano, R. J., Waters, T., & McNulty, B. A. (2005). *School leadership that works: From research to results*. Alexandria, VA: Association for Supervision and Curriculum Development.

Maslow, A. (1954). *Motivation and personality*. New York, NY: Harper.

Mayer, K. (2011) Addressing students' misconceptions about gases: Mass and composition. *Journal of Chemical Education 88*, 111–113.

McCay, L., Flora, J., Hamilton, A., & Riley, J. F. (2001). Reforming schools through teacher-leadership: A program for classroom teachers as agents of change. *Educational Horizons 79*, 135–142.

McCusker, C. (2004). *Leading a change in operating culture: What leaders must do*. Atlanta, GA.: Turknett Leadership Group.

Metropolitan Life Survey of the American Teacher. (2000). *Are we preparing students for the 21st century?* Retrieved from http://www.eric.ed.gov/PDFS/ED502263.pdf

Miller, B., Moon, J., & Elko, S. (2000). *Teacher leadership in mathematics and science: Casebook and facilitator's guide*. Portsmouth, NH: Heinemann.

Morgan, G. (1986). *Images of organization*. Newbury Park, CA: Sage Publications.

Moyo, G. 2004. *Re-inventing educational leadership for school and community transformation: Learning from the educational leadership management and development programme of the University of Fort Hare*. Unpublished Ph.D. dissertation, Rhodes University, Grahamstown, South Africa.

Murphy, J., Smylie, M., Mayrowetz, D., & Louis, K. S. (2009). The role of the principal in fostering the development of distributed leadership. *School Leadership and Management 29*(2), 181–214.

Mwangi, R. M. (2011). *School leadership, collective mindfulness and mathematics achievement in Kenya* (Doctoral dissertation, Case Western Reserve University). Retrieved from http://hdl.handle.net/2186/ksl:weaedm372/weaedm372.pdf

Năstase, M. (2010). Developing a strategic leadership approach within the organizations. *Revista de Management Comparat Internationa /Review of International Comparative Management 11*(3), 454–460.

National Education Association of New Mexico & AFT New Mexico. (2011). *2011 joint legislative goals*. Retrieved from http://www.nea-nm.org/Legislative/2011/2011JointLegGoals-FINAL.doc

Newmann, F. M., Marks, H., Louis, K., Kruse, S., & Gamoran, A. (1996). *Authentic achievement: Restructuring schools for intellectual quality*. San Francisco: Jossey-Bass.

NJEA Review. (2011, November). *Education reform done right, right now*. Retrieved from http://www.njea.org/njea-media/pdf/EdReformDoneRight.pdf?1322447833777

Norman, D. A. (1983). Some observations on mental models. In D. Gentner & A. L. Stevens (Eds.), *Mental models* (pp. 7–14). Hillsdale, NJ: Erlbaum.

Norris, C. J., & Barnett, B. (1994, October). *Cultivating a new leadership paradigm: From cohorts to communities*. Paper presented at the annual meeting of the University Council of Educational Administration, Philadelphia, PA.

Olsen, J. R. (2012). Teacher facilitator page. Retrieved from http://faculty.wiu.edu/JR-Olsen/wiu/tea/TeacherFacilitator/front.html

Olson, L. (2007, May 4). Leadership by teachers gains notice. *Education Week 26*(36), 1, 14–15. Available at http://www.edweek.org/ew/articles/2007/05/09/36teachlead.h26.html

Pajardo, P. (2011, Fall). *Principals and teachers: Partners in leadership*. Session presented at the conference of the Association for Supervision and Curriculum Development, Las Vegas, Nevada.

Papay, J. (2012). *Do supportive professional environments in schools nurture teacher development?* (Preliminary draft). Harvard Graduate School of Education, Center for Education Policy Research. Retrieved from http://www.aefpweb.org/sites/default/files/webform/

Kraft%20%26%20Papay%20Prof.%20Env.%20%26%20Teacher%20Development%20020112.pdf

Park, S., Henkin, A. B., & Egley, R. (2005). Teacher team commitment, teamwork and trust: Exploring associations. *Journal of Educational Administration 43*(5), 462–479.

Parolini, J., Patterson, K., & Winston, B. (2009). Distinguishing between transformational and servant leadership. *Leadership and Organization Development Journal 30,* 274–291.

Pausch, R. (2008). *The last lecture.* New York, NY: Hyperion.

Pellicer, I. O., & Anderson, L. W. (1995). *A handbook for teacher leaders.* Thousand Oaks, CA: Corwin Press.

Perry, A. (1908). *The management of a city school.* New York, NY: Macmillan.

Peters, A. L. (2011). (Un)planned failure: Unsuccessful succession planning in an urban district. *Journal of School Leadership 21*(1), 64–86.

PLC leader description, recruitment, and application. (2012). Retrieved from http://fsd.viadesto.com/media/EDocs/PLC_Leader_App.pdf

Popper, M. (2011). Toward a theory of followership. *Review of General Psychology 15*(1), 29–36.

Portner, H. (2001). *Training mentors is not enough.* Thousand Oaks, CA: Corwin Press.

Portner, H. (2002). *Being mentored.* Thousand Oaks, CA: Corwin Press.

Reeves, D. B. (2006, May). Of hubs, bridges, and networks. *Educational Leadership 63*(8), 32–37.

Reiss, S. (2004). Multifaceted nature of intrinsic motivation: The theory of 16 basic desires. *Review of General Psychology 8,* 179–193.

Roby, D. (2011, July). Teacher-leaders impacting school culture. *Education 131*(4), 782–790. Retrieved from http://web.ebscohost.com/

ehost/detail?sid=d5f53559-b4a5-424b-8382-275c55f5d56e%40sessionmgr112&vid=1&hid=103&bdata=JnNpdGU9ZWhvc3QtbGl2ZQ%3d%3d#db=pbh&AN=61803698

Ronfeldt, M., Loeb, S., & Wyckoff, J. (2012, March). *How teacher turnover harms student achievement.* Paper presented at the 37th Annual Association for Education Finance and Policy (AEFP) Conference, Boston, MA. Retrieved from http://blogs.edweek.org/edweek/teacherbeat/TchTrnStAch%20AERJ%20R%26R%20not%20blind.pdf

Rupp-Fulwiler, B. (2007). *Writing in science: How to scaffold instruction to support learning.* Portsmouth, NH: Heinemann.

Rupp-Fulwiler, B. (2011). *Writing in science in action: Strategies, tools, and classroom video.* Portsmouth, NH: Heinemann.

Sacken, D. (1994, May). No more principals! *Phi Delta Kappan, 75,* 664–670.

Salas, E., Sims, D. E., & Burke, C. S. (2005). Is there a big five in teamwork? *Small Group Research 36,* 555–599.

Schen, L. T., & Teddlie, C. (2008, June). A new model of school culture: A response to a call for conceptual clarity. *Journal of School Effectiveness and School Improvement 19*(2), 129–153.

Schmoker, M. (2006a). *Results now: How we can achieve unprecedented improvements in teaching and learning.* Alexandria, VA: Association for Supervision and Curriculum Development.

Schmoker, M. (2006b). *The opportunity: From "brutal facts" to the best schools we've ever had* [PowerPoint® presentation]. Retrieved from http://www.nsdc.org/connect/schmoker06.ppt

Scripture, E. W. (1897). *The new psychology.* New York, NY: Scribners.

Sebastian, J., & Allensworth, E. (2012). The influence of principal leadership on classroom instruction and student learning: A study of mediated pathways to learning. *Educational Administration Quarterly 48*(4), 626–663. Retrieved from http://eaq.sagepub.com/content/early/2012/02/09/0013161X11436273

Senge, P. (1990). *The fifth discipline*. New York, NY: Currency Doubleday.

Sergiovanni, T. J. (2001). *Leadership: What's in it for schools?* New York, NY: Routledge-Felmer.

Shen, J. (2005). *School principals*. New York, NY: Peter Lang Publishing.

Show, K., & Woo, E. (2008). Washington State's science assessment system: One district's approach to preparing teachers and students. In J. Coffey, R. Douglas, & C. Stearns (Eds.), *Assessing science learning. Perspectives from research and practice* (pp. 357–377). Arlington, VA: National Science Teachers Association.

Simmons B. L. (2010, March). The harder you push, the harder the system pushes back [Web log post]. Retrieved from http://www.bretlsimmons.com/2010-03/the-harder-you-push-the-harder-the-system-pushes-back/

Smith, P. A., & Scarbrough, C. S. (2011). Mindful schools as high-reliability organizations: The effect of trust on organizational mindfulness. In M. F. Dipaola & R. B. Forsyth (Eds.), *Leading research in educational administration: A festschrift for Wayne K. Hoy* (pp. 17–39). Charlotte, NC: Information Age Publishing.

Somnath, S., Hanuscin, D., Rebello, C., Muslu, N., & Cheng, Y. (2012). Confronting myths about teacher leadership. *European Journal of Physics Education 3*(2), 12–21.

Spillane, J. (2005). Distributed leadership. *The Educational Forum 69*(2), 143–150.

Starratt, R. J. (2004a). *Ethical leadership*. San Francisco, CA: Jossey-Bass.

Starratt, R. J. (2004b). *Responsible leadership. The educational forum 69*(2), 124–133.

Starratt, R. J. (2012). *Cultivating an ethical school*. New York, NY: Routledge.

Steinbeck, J. (1980). *Travels with Charley: In search of America*. Logan, IA: Perfection Learning.

Stronge, J. H., & Leeper, L. M. (2012). *Research synthesis of Virginia Principal Evaluation competencies and standards*. Retrieved from http://www.doe.virginia.gov/teaching/performance_evaluation/research_synthesis_of_principal_eval.pdf

Sydow, J., Lerch, F., Huxham, C., & Hibbert, P. (2011). A silent cry for leadership: Organizing for leading (in) clusters. *The Leadership Quarterly 22*(2), 328–343.

Task Force on Teacher Leadership. (2001). *Report of the Task Force on Teacher Leadership*. Retrieved from http://www.iel.org/programs/21st/reports/teachlearn.pdf

Teacher Leadership Exploratory Consortium. (2011). *Teacher leader model standards*. Retrieved from http://teacherleaderstandards.org/

Thomas, P. L. (2012). *21st century teachers: Easy to hire, easy to fire*. Retrieved from http://www.schoolsmatter.info/2012/01/21st-century-teachers-easy-to-hire-easy.html

Tighe, J., & Wiggins, G. (2005). *Understanding by design* (Expanded 2nd ed.). Boston, MA: Pearson

Timpe, K. (2008, July). Who are you[r] intellectual influences on your approach to education? [Web log comment]. Retrieved from http://www.linkedin.com/groups/Who-are-you-intellectual-influences-148975.S.63888159?view=&gid=148975&type=member&item=63888159&report.success=62WUlrnddR6bgwSqXhj6sMCT

Troen, V., & Boles, K. C. (2011a). *The power of teacher teams*. Thousand Oaks, CA: Corwin Press.

Troen, V., & Boles, K. C. (2011b). Rating your teacher team. *Harvard Education Letter 27*(6). Retrieved from http://www.hepg.org/hel/article/519#home

Tschannen-Moran, M. (2011). In search of trust: Contributing to the understanding of a taken-for-granted construct. In M. F. Dipaola & R. B. Forsyth (Eds.), *Leading research in educational administration: A festschrift for Wayne K. Hoy* (pp. 17–39). Charlotte, NC: Information Age Publishing.

United States Department of Defense, Office of the Assistant Secretary of Defense. (2002). DoD News Briefing—Secretary Rumsfeld and Gen. Myers. Retrieved 6/7/13 from www.defense.gov/transcripts/transcript. aspx?transcriptid=2636.

United States Department of Education. (2012). *The RESPECT Project: Envisioning a teaching profession for the 21st century*. Retrieved from http://www.ed.gov/teaching/national-conversation/vision

van den Bossche, P., Gijselaers, W., Segers, M., Woltjer, G., & Kirschner, P. A. (2010). Team learning: Building shared mental models. *Instructional Science 39*(3), 283–301. doi.1007/s11251- 11010-19128-11253

van Dierendonck, D. (2011). Servant leadership: A review and synthesis. *Journal of Management 37*(4), 1228–1261.

Van Houtte, M. (2005). Climate or culture: A plea for conceptual clarity in school effectiveness research. *School Effectiveness and School Improvement 16*(1), 71–89.

van Knippenberg, D., De Dreu, C. K. W., & Homan, A. C. (2004). Work group diversity and group performance: An integrative model and research agenda. *Journal of Applied Psychology 89*(6), 1008–1022.

Van Roekel, D. (2011). *Leading the profession: NEA's three-point plan for reform*. Retrieved from http://www.nea.org/assets/docs/PR_LeadingtheProfession.pdf

Wade, C., & Ferriter, B. (2007). Will you help me lead? *Educational Leadership 65*(1), 65–68.

Wahlstrom, K., & Louis, K. S. (2008). How teachers experience principal leadership: The roles of professional community, trust, efficacy and shared responsibility. *Educational Administration Quarterly 44*(4), 458–495.

Waldron, N. L., & McLeskey, J. (2010). Establishing a collaborative school culture through comprehensive school reform. *Journal of Educational and Psychological Consultation 20*, 58–74.

Wallace Foundation. (2011). *The school principal as leader: Guiding schools to better teaching and learning.* New York, NY: Author. Available from http://www.wallacefoundation.org

Walumbwa, F. O., Hartnell, C. A., & Oke, A. (2010). Servant leadership, procedural justice climate, service climate, employee attitudes, and organizational citizenship behavior: A cross-level investigation. *Journal of Applied Psychology 95*, 517–529.

Warren, R. (2002). *The purpose driven life*. Grand Rapids, MI: Zondervan.

Wasley, P. A. (1992). Working together: Teacher leadership and collaboration. In C. Livingston (Ed.), *Teacher leaders: Evolving roles* (pp. 21–55). Washington, DC: National Education Association.

Weiner, J. M. (2011). Finding common ground: Teacher leaders and principals speak out about teacher leadership. *Journal of School Leadership 21*(1), 7–41.

Weiss, C. (1992). *Shared decision making about what? A comparison of schools with and without teacher participation*. Paper presented at the annual meeting of the American Educational Research Association, San Francisco, California.

Wiseman, L. (2010). *Multipliers: How the best leaders make everyone smarter*. New York, NY: Harper Collins.

Yaron, J. (October 2009). *Shared leadership: Practice and perceptions of teachers in a virtual community* (Doctoral thesis, the Hebrew University). Retrieved from http://www.etni.org.il/judy_yaron/thesis_Judy_Yaron.pdf

York-Barr, J., & Duke, K. (2004). What do we know about teacher leadership? Findings from two decades of scholarship. *Review of Educational Research 74,* 255–316.

Yukl, G. (1999). An evaluation of conceptual weaknesses in transformational and charismatic leadership theories. *Leadership Quarterly 10,* 285–305.

Zander, R., & Zander, B. (2000). *Transforming professional and personal life: The art of possibility.* London, UK: Penguin Books.

Zepeda, S. J. (1999). *Staff development: Practices that promote leadership in learning communities.* Larchmont, NY: Eye on Education.

INDEX

A

Absolute Return for Kids (ARK), 72
Ackerman, R., 52, 78
Adams, J. Q., 54
Allensworth, E., 23
American Federation of Teachers, 50, 57
Anderson, M. G., 47
Anderson, S., 23, 26–27
Anthony, N., 49
"Are We Preparing Students for the 21st Century?," 1
Aspen Institute, 71
Assessment, 114–117
Austin Texas Independent School District, 7

B

Backup behavior, 35
Barkley, S., 92
Barth, R. S., 50, 59
Bass, B. M., 79
Beatty, D., 64
Beliefs, 51
Berg, J. H., 27
Berry, B., 42
Black, D. S., 94
Blase, J., 57, 84
Blogging, 64
Boles, K. C., 61
Boston Teacher Leadership Resource Center, 100
Bottoms, G., 92
Boyd-Dimock, V., 58
Braden, M., 46
Bradstad, T., 2
Brubaker, D. L., 45
Burke, C. S., 35
Bynum, B. H., 35

C

Capacity building, 25–26, 36–37, 106–107
Carroll, L., 10
Casavant, C., 12
Center for Collaborative Education, 113
Chaskin, R. J., 37
Clark, S., 92
Clemson-Ingram, R., 2

Clinton, D. S., 72
Cody, A., 3
Cohen, E., 72
Cohen, J., 89–90
Collaborative/collective leadership, 26–27
Collective mindfulness, 94–95
Collective responsibility/efficacy, 25
Collins, W., 12
Commission on Effective Teachers and Teaching (CETT), 66, 119
Common ground
    allowing teachers to lead, 23–24
    case study, 19–21
    celebrating wins, 22
    efficacy/responsibility, building collective, 25
    finding, 21
    mission statements, 21
    professional identification, need to expand, 22–23
    roles, overlapping, 25, 26
    school capacity, 25–26
    vantage point and perspective, 24–25
Concordia University, 70–71
Consortium for Excellence in Teacher Education, 7
Cool Cat Teacher Blog, 43
Cooper, G. R., 12
Cortez-Ford, E., 114
Cosner, S., 85
Costa, A., 48–49
Covey, S., 10, 103, 105, 106
Crevani, L., 78

D

Danielson, C., 2, 3, 56, 58, 76, 78, 86
Davis, V., 43
Deal, T., 99
De Dreu, C.K.W., 34
Denhardt, J., 105
Denhardt, R., 105
De Pree, M., 88
Deuel, A., 78–79
Devos, G., 81

Distributive leadership, 93, 95–96
District or community issues, 63–66
Donaldson, G. A., Jr., 87
Donaldson, M. L., 77
Drucker, P., 95
DuFour, R., 59
Duignan, P., 12
Duke, K., 28–29

E
Early, D., 105
Educational Leadership Constituent
    Council (ELCC), 6
Efficacy, building collective, 25
Egley, R., 35
Elmore, R. F., 62
Empowerment. *See* Shared leadership
Enlightened leadership, 78
Erickson, L., 19
Ethics, 100–101
Evans, R., 102
Expectations, 51

F
Facilitators, 44
Faginski, E., 12
Fairman, J. C., 47
Feagin, C. H., 92
Fege, A., 90
Fennel, M., 66
Ferriter, B., 60, 77–78
Fessler, R., 2
Fink, D., 102
Fink, S., 63
Ford Foundation, 7
Formal leadership, 46, 55
Fullan, M., 25, 100, 101, 106, 107
Future Leaders, 72

G
Gates, B., 30
GE, 72
Gijselaers, W., 34
Giles, C., 107
Glover, E., 78
Goals, what we know versus what
    we do, 10–11
Goddard, R. D., 25
Goddard, Y. L., 25

Goldring, E., 12
Goodson, I., 106
Grant, C., 95
Greenleaf, R., 104
Groups versus teams, 34
Gulledge, K. A., 106

H
Hackney, C. E., 6
Hallinger, P., 26, 85
Hargreaves, A., 102, 106, 107
Harris, A., 36–37, 86, 93, 95, 96, 109
Harrison, C., 57, 86
Hattie, J., 13
Heck, R. H., 26, 85
Heifetz, R., 12, 23, 102
Henderson, J. G., 6
Henkin, A. B., 35
Hibbert, P., 79
Hirsch, E., 114
Hirsch, S. A., 61–62, 114
Hirsh, S., 70
Hoffman, B. J., 35
Homan, A. C., 34
Hopkins, D., 95
Hord, S. M., 61–62
Hoy, W. K., 94
Hulpia, H., 81
Huxham, C., 79

I
Informal leadership, 3, 46, 55, 100
Ingersoll, R., 116
Instructional leadership, 13, 31
Interstate School Leaders Licensure
    Consortium (ISLLC), 6, 69
Iwanicki, E. F., 47

J
Johnson, S. M., 77
Jones, M. F., 105
*Journal of Research for Educational
    Leaders*, 6
Juechter, W. M., 33
Juvonen, J., 60

K
Kallick, B., 48–49
Katzenbach, J. R., 34

Kelley, J. D., 68
Kelly, E., 47
Kempher, L., 12
Killion, J., 57, 87
Kirschner, P. A., 34
Knight, J., 28
Knowledge Is Power Program
    (KIPP), 7–8
Kouzes, J. M., 45

L

Lacey, K., 108
Lambert, L., 4–5, 36–37, 61, 95–96
Lamoureax, K., 72
Leadership
    See also Shared leadership;
      Teacher-leaders
    allowing teachers to take, 23–24
    collaborative/collective, 26–27
    continuum, 79–80
    density, 5
    distributive, 93, 95–96
    enlightened, 78
    formal, 46, 55
    heroic view of, problem with,
      78–79
    informal, 3, 46, 55, 100
    Lambert's critical factors of, 4–5
    programs at universities, 7, 70–71
    reframing perceptions of, 95–96
    servant, 104–105
    structuration view of, 79
    styles, 12
    top-down, 1
    training, 6–8
    transformational versus transactional,
      79–80
    types, 13, 31
Leadership Institute of Riverside
    County (LIRC), 71
Leading for Instructional Improvement
    (Fink and Markholt), 63
Leana, C. R., 2
Leeper, L. M., 12, 13, 88, 91
Leithwood, K., 23, 26–27, 95
Lerch, F., 79
Lindgren, M., 78
Linton, K., 49–50
Lipson, M. Y., 99
Living systems, 101
Loeb, S., 115

Lord, B., 55, 57
Louis, K., 23, 25, 26–27, 96, 103
Lukwago, M., 64

M

Mackenzie, S. V., 47, 52, 78
Mandela, N., 99
Margolis, J. M., 43, 78–79
Markholt, A., 63
Marks, H. M., 30–31
Marks, M. A., 35
Marzano, R., 14, 24, 84
Mascall, B., 27
Maslow, A., 47, 51
Math and Science Leadership Academy
    (MSLA), 56
Mathieu, J. E., 35
Mayrowetz, D., 103
McCabe, E. M., 89–90
McCandless, J., 12
McCusker, C., 36
McGree, K. M., 58
McLeskey, J., 25
McNulty, B. A., 14, 24, 84
Mekkelsen, J., 99
Mental models, 34
Mentorship programs, 57, 73
*Metropolitan Life Survey of the
    American Teacher*, 1
Michelli, N. M., 89–90
Milagro Beanfield War, The, 31
Miller, B., 55, 57
Mindfulness, collective, 94–95
Mission statements, 21
Model Standards for Teacher Leadership,
    44, 69, 122–125
Montgomery County Public Schools
    (MCPS), 7
Morgan, G., 4
Mosenthal, J. H., 99
Murphy, J., 103, 104
Mwangi, R. M., 94

N

Năstase, M., 84
National College, 72
National Education Association,
    50, 57, 66
Networks, 64–66
New Jersey Education Association, 73
Norman, D. A., 34

O

Ohio Department of Education, 7
Olsen, J. R., 44
Open Letter to President Obama
    (Cody), 3
*Opportunity: From "Brutal Facts" to the
    Best Schools We've Ever Had, The*
    (Schmoker), 20

P

Packendorff, J., 78
Pajardo, P., 68
Papay, J., 114
Park, S., 35
Pasteur, L., 10
Pausch, R., 36
Peers, working with, 56–58
Penn State, 7, 71
Perry, A., 90
Perspective, role of, 24–25
Peters, A. L., 100, 102, 108–109
Peterson, K. D., 99
Philadelphia Education Fund, 71–72
Piccolo, R. F., 35
Pickeral, T., 89–90
Portner, H., 48, 51
Posner, B. Z., 45
Principals
    changing school and role of, 90–92
    coping with changing role of, 12
    professional identification, need to
        expand, 22–23
    responsibilities of, 13–14, 23, 24
    role and use of term, 1–2
    teams and role of, 61–63
Printy, S. M., 30–31
Professional identification, need to
    expand, 22–23
Professional learning communities
    (PLCs), 59–61, 96

R

Report of the Task Force on Teacher
    Leadership, 50
Restructuring, 100
Rewards, 51
Roby, D., 5
Roles, overlapping, 25, 26
Ronfeldt, M., 115
Rumsfeld, D., 76
Russ, B., 99

S

Sacks, A., 44
Salas, E., 35
Samford University, 7
Sanctuary, finding a, 102
Scarbrough, C. S., 94
Schen, L. T., 88, 89
Schmoker, M., 11, 20, 83
School-based groups, working with, 58–61
School capacity, 25–26, 85
School climate, defined, 88–89
School culture, 3–4
    case studies, 81–83
    changing, and role of principals, 90–92
    defined, 88–90
    distributive leadership, 93, 95–96
    failures/mistakes, handling, 81–82
    mindfulness, collective, 94–95
    separating practice from practitioner, 96–97
    shaping, 76–87
    small wins, 83–84
    situational awareness, 84–85
    trust building, 84, 93–94
    unity, building, 92
    "us" versus "them" mentality, 77–78
Schools Matter, 64
Sebastian, J., 23
Segers, M., 34
Self-actualization, 47
Self-renewal, 102–104
Senge, P., 12, 34
Sergiovanni, T. J., 5, 14
Servant leadership, 104–105
7 Habits of Highly Effective People, The
    (Covey), 10
Shared leadership, 2
    case studies, 14–17, 32–33, 37–39
    changing views of, 12–14, 31–32
    cultivating, 30–31
    experiences, role of, 32
    teamwork, 33–35
    trust, 35–36
Sharpening the saw, 103
Sherif, G., 72
Simmons, B. L., 12–13
Sims, D. E., 35
Situational awareness, 84–85
Smith, D. K., 34
Smith, P. A., 94
Smylie, M., 103
Spillane, J., 78, 79, 80

Standards, 44, 69–70, 122–125
Starratt, R. J., 100–101, 105
State license endorsements, 72–73
Steinbeck, J., 32
Stewardship, 103
Strong, M., 116
Stronge, J. H., 12, 13, 88, 91
Student achievement, principals and, 14, 24
Succession planning, 108–109
Sustainability
    barriers to, 107
    benefits of, 102–103
    building, 99–110
    case studies, 109–110
    defined, 105–107
    different perspectives, importance of, 108
    ethical implications, 100–101
    self-renewal, 102–104
    servant leadership, 104–105
    succession planning, 108–109
    systemic approach, 101
Sutton, A. W., 35
Sydow, J., 79
Synergy, 90
Systematic approach, 101
Systemic approach, 101

T
Tarter, C. J., 94
Teacher-leaders
    barriers to, 47–51
    characteristics of, 51–52
    in classrooms, 44–45
    conditions necessary for, 86–87
    defined, 42–44
    development programs, 7, 70–72
    district or community issues and, 63–66
    evaluating/assessing, 114–117
    examples, 54–55
    formal, 46, 55
    helping, to help themselves, 95
    informal, 3, 46, 55
    lite, 80–81
    mentoring future, 73
    motivation, 47
    networks, 64–66
    research, 26–29
    role of, 2
    school practices and policies and, 55–63
    standards, 69–70
    state license endorsements, 72–73

unions and, 50
    working with peers, 56–58
    working with school-based groups, 58–61
Teacher Leadership Exploratory Consortium,
    69, 71, 120–121
Teacher Leadership for Urban Schools, 7
Teacher Leadership Resource Center (TLRC)
    (Boston), 70
Teacher-Leaders Network (TLN), 3, 65
Teacherpreneurs, 43–44
Teach First, 72
Teaching Leaders, 72
Teaching Policy Fellowship, 65
Teams
    departmental, 61
    interdisciplinary, 60
    leadership issues, 61
    principals and, 61–63
Teamwork, 33–35
Teddlie, C., 88, 89
Telecommunications Systems Inc., 72
Tencza, M., 12
Textron, 72
Thomas, P. L., 64
Tichy, N., 72
Tighe, J., 10
Timpe, K., 8
Trait theory, 96
Transactional leadership, 79–80
Transformational leadership, 13, 31, 79–80
Travels with Charley: In Search of America
    (Steinbeck), 32
Troen, V., 61
Trust, 35–36, 84, 93–94
Tschannen-Moran, M., 93–94

U
Understanding by Design (Tighe and
    Wiggins), 10
Unions, role of, 50
Unity, building, 92
University of Central Florida, 7
University of Cincinnati, 7

V
van den Bossche, P., 34
Van Houtte, M., 88, 89
Van Keer, H., 81
van Knippenberg, D., 34
Van Roekel, D., 63, 66
Vantage point and perspective, 24–25

W

Wade, C., 77–78
Wahlstrom, K., 23, 25, 26–27, 96
Waldron, N. L., 25
Wallace Foundation, 13–14, 85
Walumbwa, F. O., 105
Warren, R., 110
Waters, T., 14, 24, 84
Waters of Ayole, The, 28
Weiner, J. M., 27–28
Welch, J., 72
Wiggins, G., 10

Wiseman, L., 12
Woltjer, G., 34
Wyckoff, J., 115

Y

Yaron, J., 45
York-Barr, J., 28–29
Yukl, G., 79

Z

Zaccaro, S. J., 35
Zander, B., 23–24
Zander, R. S., 23–24